Tapas

hamlyn

Tapas

80 of the best recipes

Joanna Farrow

Notes

Ovens should be preheated to the specified temperature. If using a fan-assisted oven, follow the manufacturer's instructions for adjusting the time and temperature. Grills should also be preheated.

This book includes dishes made with nuts and nut derivatives. It is advisable for those with known allergic reactions to nuts and nut derivatives and those who may be potentially vulnerable to these allergies, such as pregnant women and nursing mothers, invalids, the elderly, babies and children, to avoid dishes made with nuts and nut oils. It is also prudent to check the labels of preprepared ingredients for the possible inclusion of nut derivatives.

The Department of Health advises that eggs should not be consumed raw. This book contains some dishes made with raw or lightly cooked eggs. It is prudent for more vulnerable people, such as pregnant women and nursing mothers, invalids, the elderly, babies and young children to avoid uncooked or lightly cooked dishes made with eggs.

Fresh herbs should be used unless otherwise stated. If unavailable use dried herbs as an alternative but halve the quantities stated.

Meat and poultry should be cooked thoroughly. To test if poultry is cooked, pierce the flesh through the thickest part with a skewer or fork – the juices should run clear, never pink or red.

An Hachette Livre UK Company

First published in Great Britain in 2008 by
Hamlyn, a division of Octopus Publishing Group Ltd
2–4 Heron Quays, London E14 4JP
www.octopusbooks.co.uk

Copyright © Octopus Publishing Group Ltd 2008

Distributed in the U.S. and Canada for Octopus
Books USA by:
Hachette Book Group USA
237 Park Avenue
New York NY 10017

ISBN: 978-0-600-61737-2

A CIP catalogue record for this book is available
from the British Library

Printed and bound in China

10 9 8 7 6 5 4 3 2 1

Contents

Introduction *In Spain, tapas are eaten both at lunchtime and during the evening. They embody a relaxed, sociable aspect of daily life, and bars throng with activity as customers whet their appetites with the feast on offer, both traditional and more contemporary.*

In larger towns and cities, to go on a tapeo *(tapas bar crawl) is the norm, as people seek out the house specialities of the various bars. These might take the form of hot dishes made to order or a buffet-style array of food laid out at the bar. Tapas can be as simple as a snack of olives, nuts, cheese or cured meats, or they can be more elaborate, fascinating little tasters of hot or cold dishes, served as finger food or in little* cazuelas, *the traditional Spanish terracotta dishes. Although there's a vast range of regional tapas, derived from local and seasonal produce, almost any foods served in suitably small dishes (so there's always room to eat more) can be described as tapas.*

They originated in the custom of serving a simple slice of bread, cold meat or cheese with a drink, often to stave off hunger for the farm workers. This custom has now reached great culinary heights, adopted by bars, clubs and restaurants throughout Europe and beyond, and it adapts well to relaxed entertaining at home.

Tapas-style entertaining

As in bars and restaurants, you can serve either a light selection of nibbles before a main meal or a more extensive range of dishes that might take the place of a meal altogether. (The Spanish sometimes eat their main meal at lunchtime, with tapas as their meal in the evening.) If you're serving pre-dinner tapas, keep the choice simple. Marinated olives, slivers of cheese or ham, salted almonds and a couple of hot or cold tapas dishes are all you will need, without running the risk of everyone overindulging before dinner. This can conveniently take the place of a starter.

If you have decided to serve tapas as a meal in themselves, prepare a larger assortment of hot and cold dishes, but avoid the risk over 'over catering' – you don't want to spend the whole evening in the kitchen. Tapas are ideal, of course, for eating at the garden table on a hot summer's evening, but they needn't become a 'sit-down' meal unless you find this easier. Many dishes can be served as finger food, in the style of a drinks party, so you can leave the food on trays so that everyone can help themselves. Make the occasion easier

by bearing in mind the following:

• Serve two or three uncooked tapas first. These dishes might include some salted almonds, marinated olives or anchovies, or a selection of cold meats or cheese.

• Some good quality, rustic bread or tasty Mediterranean-style bread can be served for mopping up sauces and dressings or dipping in good quality olive oil.

• Follow with a few cold tapas that you have prepared in advance and have stored, wrapped in clingfilm, in the refrigerator or a cool place. A good selection might include meat and fish tapas as well as cheese or vegetable ones.

• Finish with two or three hot tapas. Most of the recipes in this book can be prepared ahead so there's little last-minute cooking.

• It can be difficult to estimate portion sizes. As a guide, a stack of three of four little fritters or bite-sized pieces of food constitutes a portion.

• Keep a good balance of easy and more time-consuming recipes and have as much prepared in advance as possible.

• Mix up colours, flavours and textures so that you offer your guests a feast of different taste sensations.

Serving tapas

Tapas dining is casual, relaxed and sociable, and the way the dishes are served should reflect this. The easiest option is to use platters and large plates or dishes so that everyone can dip in. If you are serving tapas as finger food, all you will need is a stack of napkins for mopping up. If the dishes need forks, use small tea plates or even saucers.

The portions should be taster sized – this is not a main meal, after all – and small dishes will discourage people from taking too much! Alternatively, serve the tapas plated up in single portions. *Cazuelas* (traditional earthenware dishes) are fairly widely available but almost any other small dishes can be used, including little ramekins or even small cereal bowls.

What to drink with tapas

Bearing in mind that tapas and drinking go hand in hand, you might want to consider extending the choice of drinks to include more than simply red or white wine. Beer, sherry and *sidra* (Spanish cider) are as much a part of the ritual as the food.

Ultimately, it's important to drink what you like, whether it's breaking the rules or not, but it would be a shame not to keep to Spanish drinks for authenticity.

The lightest, freshest sherries, such as Manzanilla and Fino, served very chilled, are great aperitifs and good with almost any tapas. For those who prefer a more full-bodied sherry, there's Amontillado or Oloroso, which might better suit richer, meatier tapas dishes or be offered to complement very salty dishes. The richest, sweetest sherries are the Moscatel and Pedro Ximenez, which are more in the league of dessert wines.

Serve any Spanish red or white wines. Rioja is still the best known and leading wine region, but almost every other region of Spain produces and exports its own distinctive wines. For a sparkling wine, particularly during the summer, try a thoroughly chilled, good quality Cava.

Cider is another favourite to be served with tapas, and its slightly sour, refreshing sparkle is perfect with salty dishes and richer ones that include cheese, seafood and meat.

Ingredients

Authentic Spanish ingredients are becoming more widely available in specialist food shops, delicatessens and supermarkets. The following all crop up frequently and are essential for good results. If you can't get them locally, it's worth searching the internet for mail order companies, which are often the easiest way to source the real thing. The quality of many Spanish food products is controlled by the Denominaciones de Origen (Designation of Origin), which guarantees good quality.

Almonds

These are used extensively in both sweet and savoury dishes and are an integral part of Spanish cuisine. Many recipes use ground almonds, which can be bought ready prepared, although for maximum flavour you should use whole almonds and grind them before use. If they are unblanched – that is, if they are in their papery brown skins – soak them in boiling water for 4–5 minutes, then drain and peel away the skins before grinding. The best-known Spanish almonds are Marcona, which are flat, round and full flavoured. Almonds are a tapas essential, either lightly toasted or salted (see page 21).

Bread

Authentic Spanish bread is difficult for most of us to obtain, so use any well-flavoured, densely textured, country-style bread. For recipes served on toast – such as Cabrales with Honey and Walnuts (see pages 26–27) and Tomato and Garlic Bread (see pages 32–33) – a small, compact loaf is best so the cut slices are not too large.

Cheeses

Manchego is by far the most internationally renowned Spanish cheese, but there are many others that deserve the same recognition. Their character is determined by climate and by the grazing and type of milk used. The wetter climate of northern

Spain produces Cabrales and Valdeon (also known as Picos de Europa), two distinctive blue-veined cheeses that develop a stronger flavour as they mature. Manchego from La Mancha in central Spain is a pasteurized, hard or semi-hard ewes' milk cheese with a slightly spicy, tangy flavour. Idiazabal is made from ewes' milk and comes from Navarre in the Basque country. Nutty in flavour, it is available both smoked and unsmoked. Smooth, creamy and mild Tetilla is a cows' milk cheese from Galicia. A popular tapas choice, it's also good for melting. Of the many goats' cheeses, Cabra al Romero from Murcia is one of the better known ones, easily recognized by its thick coating of rosemary leaves.

Any cheese can be served as tapas, either individually or as a selection. They're often accompanied with something sweet, such as membrillo (see page 10), but fruity chutneys and jams or slices of pressed dried fruit 'cakes' also make good partners.

Cured meats

Pork, which is by far the most widely used meat in Spanish cooking, is taken from two very different breeds: the Iberian pigs and the European white pigs. The *cerdo iberico* (Iberian pigs), related to the Mediterranean wild boar, produce some of the tastiest and most expensive Spanish cured meats. These pigs live in the *dehesa* or light oak forests of southwestern Spain and thrive on a diet rich in acorns, weeds and roots, supplemented by cereals during the summer. Iberian ham is world renowned and is usually eaten as it is, at room temperature, to appreciate its full flavour.

Serrano ham comes from European white pigs. Less expensive than *cerdo iberico*, it can be served thinly sliced or used in cooked recipes, such as Rabbit with Serrano Ham and Sage (see page 78). Lomo is whole marinated pork loin, seasoned and dried in natural skins. It looks very like sausage, but on slicing, reveals pure, lean meat. This can be produced from Iberian and white pigs.

One of the key flavours in Spanish tapas dishes is chorizo, and there are many different types. All are pork based, occasionally with additional meats, such as beef or venison. Flavoured with garlic, spices and herbs, chorizo can be chunky or fine, thick or thin and mild or hot in flavour. Firm chorizo can be sliced thinly and eaten like salami or cooked in hot tapas dishes, its spicy, garlicky flavour permeating all the other ingredients. Soft

chorizo is almost paste like and is usually cooked before eating.

There are also many different types of morcilla, a Spanish black pudding and another spicy flavoured tapas essential. This is usually cooked and used in hot tapas dishes.

Salchichon is a coarse-cut sausage, seasoned with salt and pepper but without additional spices. Try skinning sausages before use. If the skin is thick and papery, it will probably come away easily, but if it is so fine that you can't get a grip on it, it's probably not worth trying.

Membrillo

This thick, sweet quince paste is bought in little tubs or slabs, and it can be scooped or sliced for serving with cheese, particularly hard ewes' milk cheeses, like Manchego.

Olives

Unripe olives are green and slightly bitter, but they turn black, sweeter and oilier as they ripen. The choice of olive is subjective, and there's a Spanish olive for everyone. Look out for the sweet green Manzanilla olives, large Gordals, tiny Arbequinas and black Aragon olives. Many are also available pitted and stuffed with ingredients such as anchovies, peppers, chillies, garlic and almonds. Olives preserved in olive oil (often with spices and herbs as well) tend to be more succulent, but brined olives will keep for longer and are good for marinating (see page 34).

Olive oil

Spain is the world's largest producer of olive oil and hundreds of different varieties of olive are grown, most of which go into oil production. As with olives, the oils range from tangy and slightly bitter to sweet and fruity. Extra virgin olive oil, from the first cold pressing, is the most expensive and is best reserved for table use, aïoli, dressings, marinades, chilled soups, salads and vegetable dishes, when the flavour can be appreciated. A good quality extra virgin olive oil served in small dishes with bread for breaking and dipping into the oil is a really simple form of tapas. For general cooking and deep-frying, use a regular or blended olive oil to give your tapas dishes an authentic Mediterranean flavour. All olive oils should be stored in a cool, dark place.

Paprika

Paprika is one of the most regularly used spices in Spanish cooking, its fabulous colour and flavour adding a vibrant glow and spicy warmth to so many tapas dishes. Many brands of paprika are packed in highly decorated little tins, and it's difficult to resist buying them for this alone. There are two main types: mild sweet paprika (dulce) and the spicier hot paprika (picante), which has much more of a kick. Both mild and hot paprika are also available with a deep smoky flavour, a process that originated in La Vera, a region in western Spain. Although the recipes stipulate which to use, the choice is a matter of personal taste, and they are interchangeable. Some also have a stunning depth of colour, and a little sprinkling over any tapas dish will bring it to life.

Peppers

Fresh green peppers add a crisp tang and bite to salads, while red peppers are more mellow and sweet and are often roasted before use. Small green Padron peppers from Galicia make perfect bite-sized tapas and carry the distinction that one in a large handful will have a chilli-hot bite! Dried peppers are blackened and crinkled and are great for adding an authentic flavour to cooked tapas dishes. Like the fresh type, they vary in flavour intensity. The Guindilla is hot and spicy, while the milder Nora is frequently used in Romesco Sauce (see page 35). Peppers preserved in sweet or sharp pickles make conveniently easy tapas: simply tip them out into a dish as you would olives. The Guindilla variety are most often used in this way.

Piquillo peppers are the little cone-shaped peppers, grown in the Navarre region of Spain and sold in jars or cans after slow roasting and skinning. Their shape, sweet flavour and deep red colour make them perfect for stuffing with meat, fish, cheese or vegetables. If you can't get hold of them, use another type of preserved whole pepper or, better still, whole roast fresh red peppers, cooked in a hot oven for about 40 minutes, then cooled, deseeded and skinned, ready for use.

Preserved fish

Although we may be increasingly wary of many processed foods, preserved fish and seafood, such as anchovies, tuna, sardines, baby squid, clams and mussels, feature frequently on the tapas menu and make an incredibly useful, easy serving option. Look for good quality brands, packed in Spain in olive oil (rather than vegetable oil) or rich tomato sauces. Once tipped out of the tins or jars you can easily liven them up with a sprinkling of parsley or capers and a squeeze of lemon.

Salt cod, one of the earliest forms of preserved fish, is another tapas favourite. Choose pieces that are chunky and reasonably white, rather than dark or yellowing. Soak the cod, ideally for 48 hours, changing the water frequently, although you might get away with a 24-hour soaking if you are using a particularly good quality salt cod.

Rice

Spain produces a range of different types of rice, but it is short grain paella rice for which the country is best known. Highly absorbent, the rice soaks up all the flavours of the ingredients it's cooked with and turns slightly sticky, perfect for the Paella Cakes on page 109.

Saffron

Spain is the world's leading producer of saffron and, although it's extremely expensive, a little goes a long way. Use it to add that essential Mediterranean glow, flavour and warm, unique aroma to many tapas dishes. Harvesting saffron is a highly specialized and labour-intensive business. Each crocus flower is carefully picked, and from these the three stigmas are removed and dried. It takes around 80,000 of these to make up 500 g (1 lb) of saffron, hence its colossal price. As a guide, the redder the colour the better the quality, and saffron from La Mancha is generally considered the best. Buy saffron in small quantities and store in a cool dry place.

Sherry

Sherry comes from Andalusia in southern Spain, and production centres around the town of Jerez de la Frontera, from which it takes its name. Most is produced from the Palomino vine, with a small amount from Pedro Ximinez and Moscatel. From light, crisp, dry sherries to sweet, full-bodied cream ones, all can be cooked with or served with tapas, and the choice comes down to personal preference. Sherry is particularly good in dishes like Rabbit with Serrano Ham and Sage (see page 78) or Chorizo with New Potatoes (see page 66), when it's reduced to a syrupy consistency with an intense flavour and lively kick.

Store sherry in a cool place and buy half bottles if you won't be using a large amount because it doesn't keep indefinitely.

Sherry vinegar

A good quality, well-aged sherry vinegar can be used in much the same way as an Italian balsamic vinegar, adding a resonant tang to dressings, sauces and cooked dishes. As with balsamic, prices vary considerably.

Basic techniques

Here are some basic preparation techniques that crop up repeatedly in tapas recipes.

Peeling raw prawns

Pinch off the heads and then peel away the shell and tail. If liked, you can leave the ends of the tails intact to act as handles if you're going to serve the prawns as finger food. If there's a black, thread-like intestine running along the back or underside of the prawn, remove it by making a small cut along the prawn and pulling away the thread.

Preparing seafood

As far as possible, buy shellfish on the day you intend to use it. There's no need to soak mussels and clams in a bowl of water in the refrigerator as it does not help to keep them fresh.

Mussels

Wash mussels in plenty of cold water to remove all traces of grit and seaweed. Scrape off any barnacles with a knife

and pull away the beards. These are the seaweed-like threads that the mussels use to cling to rocks and ropes. As you clean them, check that all the shells are intact, discarding any that are cracked or damaged. Any mussels that are open should close when tapped sharply against the side of the sink. Discard any that don't close.

Clams

Although they are less gritty and barnacled than mussels, you'll still need to check over clams, discarding any damaged or stubbornly open shells. After cooking, discard any shells that remain closed.

Scallops

Scallops are usually bought ready prepared, but they are easy to open if you buy them in their shells for use in a recipe like Scallops with Morcilla (see pages 106–7). Place them on a chopping board with the flat shell uppermost and slide the blade of a sturdy knife between the two shells on the opposite side to the hinge. Run the knife against the flat top shell so you can sever the meat from the shell. Discard everything except the coral and white muscle flesh.

Squid

Most squid can be bought ready prepared, either as the body tubes alone or cleaned with the heads and tentacles popped back into the tubes. Larger squid are also available ready sliced into rings. If you buy them unprepared, pull away the head and tentacles from the body, then scoop out and discard the contents of the body, including the transparent, plastic-like quill.

Pull off and discard the inky skin – this usually rubs off very easily with your fingers. The fins on either side of the body can be removed for cooking separately or left attached. Remove the tentacles from the head by cutting just in front of the eyes so the tentacles remain in one piece. Discard the heads. If the recipe requires, slice the body into rings. Dry all the pieces thoroughly and chill until ready to cook. Whole or prepared squid freezes well, as long as it has not previously been frozen.

Skinning tomatoes

Put the tomatoes in a bowl and cover with plenty of boiling water. Leave until the skins split. This might be less than a minute for very ripe tomatoes but 2–3 minutes if they're firmer and not quite so ripe and juicy. Pour away the water and cover with cold water. Peel away the skins with your fingers.

Quick bites *The simplicity of the tapas in this chapter shows just how, with minimal time and effort, you can assemble some absolutely delicious dishes. Some of the ideas are barely recipes at all, but rather an arrangement of well-chosen ingredients that whet the appetite for what's to follow. Serve quick bites either as pre-dinner nibbles with drinks, in place of a starter or as part of a complete tapas meal. Most are served cold, so you can prepare them in advance. The only 'extra' you might want to offer your guests is some well-flavoured, rustic bread, which always seems to disappear, along with everything else!*

Banderillas

The Spanish word banderilla *means 'barbed dart', and skewers threaded with olives, gherkins, baby onions and other strong-flavoured appetizers can be bought in jars from supermarkets and delicatessens. For more flexibility of ingredients you can make your own using cocktail sticks or slightly more ornate skewers.*

PREPARATION TIME: 10 minutes

MAKES: 20

2 piquillo or other roasted peppers

65 g (2½ oz) gherkins

20 pitted black or green olives, or Marinated Olives (see page 34)

50 g (2 oz) thinly sliced chorizo, salchichon or lomo

1 Cut the peppers and gherkins into 20 bite-sized pieces.

2 Thread a piece of each ingredient on to a skewer or cocktail stick, folding the meat in half or quarters, depending on size.

3 Arrange the skewers on a plate, cover and keep in a cool place until ready to serve.

Fig and Serrano wraps
These little morsels combine salty Serrano ham, sweet quince paste and spicy black pepper in one delicious bite. Make them several hours in advance and chill, covered in clingfilm, until ready to serve.

PREPARATION TIME: 10 minutes

MAKES: 12

3 fresh figs

40 g (1½ oz) membrillo (see page 10)

50 g (2 oz) cream cheese

½ teaspoon freshly ground black pepper

12 wafer-thin slices of Serrano ham

1 Quarter the figs. Soften the membrillo by mashing it in a small bowl if it is very firm. Add the cream cheese and pepper and mix together.

2 Arrange the ham slices on the work surface and place a spoonful of the cream cheese mixture in the centre of each one, spreading it slightly with the back of a spoon.

3 Place a fig quarter across the cream cheese mixture. Fold the ham over the fig quarter to enclose it. Arrange the little parcels on a serving plate and grind over a little extra black pepper.

Fried green peppers

This recipe shows just how delicious the simplest tapas can be. Traditionally, tiny green peppers from Padron in northern Spain are used. Because these aren't widely available, you might want to try using other small, sweet peppers.

PREPARATION TIME: 5 minutes

COOKING TIME: 5 minutes

SERVES: 6

500 g (1 lb) small green Padron peppers, left whole

4 tablespoons olive oil

sea salt

1 Wash the peppers and dry them thoroughly on kitchen paper.

2 Heat the oil in a frying pan until very hot. Add the peppers and cook quickly for about 5 minutes, turning them frequently in the oil until they blister and begin to char.

3 Transfer the peppers to a dish with a slotted spoon and serve generously sprinkled with sea salt.

Manchego with membrillo

Spain's most internationally known cheese is often paired with membrillo, a thick, sweet quince paste that contrasts perfectly with the cheese in flavour and texture.

PREPARATION TIME: 5 minutes

SERVES: 4–6

250 g (8 oz) Manchego cheese

50 g (2 oz) membrillo

1 Cut the cheese into thin, bite-sized pieces and arrange them on a platter or put 2–3 slices on individual plates.

2 Cut the membrillo into thin slices and arrange them on top of the cheese. Wrap and keep in a cool place until ready to serve.

Salted almonds
Almonds are an abundant Spanish ingredient and are used extensively in both sweet and savoury recipes. This oven-roasted, salty, spicy recipe is irresistibly easy and perfect with almost any drinks.

PREPARATION TIME: 5 minutes

COOKING TIME: 8 minutes

MAKES: 200 g (7 oz)

oil, for brushing

2 teaspoons egg white

200 g (7 oz) whole unblanched almonds

8 g (⅓ oz) sea salt

¼ teaspoon hot smoked paprika (optional)

1 Lightly brush a baking sheet with oil. Whisk the egg white with a fork in a bowl, add the almonds and mix together until coated.

2 Lightly crush the sea salt in a polythene bag with a rolling pin until finely ground.

3 Add the salt to the nuts with the paprika (if used) and toss together until well coated. Spread the nuts in a single layer on the baking sheet and cook in a preheated oven, 220°C (425°F), Gas Mark 7, for 6–8 minutes until golden. Leave them to cool on the baking sheet then tip them into a bowl. Salted almonds can be stored in an airtight container for up to 2 days.

Goats' cheese in tarragon dressing

Use any ripe but firm goats' cheese for this recipe. The dish will keep well in a cool place for several hours before serving, but avoid putting it in the refrigerator.

PREPARATION TIME: 10 minutes

SERVES: 6

150 g (5 oz) goats' cheese

5 g (¼ oz) each of tarragon, parsley and chives

3 tablespoons extra virgin olive oil

squeeze of lemon juice

1 small garlic clove, chopped

salt and pepper

1 Cut the cheese into small cubes and transfer them to a bowl.

2 Discard any tough stalks from the herbs. Roughly chop the leaves and put them in a food processor with the oil, lemon juice, garlic and salt and pepper. Blend briefly until the herbs are finely chopped, scraping any mixture down from the sides of the bowl.

3 Spoon the herb mixture over the cheese and mix well. Turn the cheese into a serving dish and cover with clingfilm until ready to serve.

Artichoke hearts with lemon and mint

This is a great way of dressing up canned artichoke hearts. Unlike fresh artichokes, they're available all year but benefit from being spruced up with some fresh Mediterranean flavours.

PREPARATION TIME: 10 minutes, plus drying and chilling

COOKING TIME: 5 minutes

SERVES: 4

400 g (13 oz) can or jar artichoke hearts

4 tablespoons extra virgin olive oil

1 garlic clove, crushed

finely grated rind of 1 lemon, plus 1 tablespoon juice

½ teaspoon caster sugar

2 tablespoons chopped mint

salt and pepper

1 Thoroughly drain the artichokes and dry them by arranging them, upside down, on several layers of kitchen paper. Leave for about 10 minutes, then cut into thin slices.

2 Heat 2 tablespoons of the oil in a frying pan and fry the artichokes for about 3 minutes until they are beginning to brown. Turn them over and scatter with the garlic, lemon rind, sugar and mint. Cook for a further couple of minutes.

3 Turn the artichokes into a serving dish or 4 small dishes. Pour the remaining oil and the lemon juice into the pan with a little salt and pepper and stir, off the heat, until mixed. Pour over the artichokes and chill for a couple of hours before serving.

Green olive paste
Rather like a tapenade, this well-flavoured paste can be spread on to little toasts or served in bowls with slices of warm bread as an accompaniment. Black olives can be substituted for the green if you prefer.

PREPARATION TIME: 5 minutes

COOKING TIME: 2 minutes

SERVES: 6

1 teaspoon coriander seeds

1 teaspoon cumin seeds

4 tablespoons olive oil

1 garlic clove, crushed

150 g (5 oz) pitted green olives

several sprigs of parsley

1 teaspoon lemon juice

salt and pepper

1 Grind the coriander and cumin seeds as finely as possible. Put them in a small saucepan with the oil and garlic and heat gently for 2 minutes.

2 Tip the spice mixture into a food processor and add the olives, parsley, lemon juice and a little salt and pepper.

3 Blend to a paste, scraping the mixture down from the sides of the bowl. Check the seasoning, then turn the paste into a small serving dish. Cover and chill until needed.

Fresh herb oil
This simple dressing is used as a garnish for spooning over some of the cooked tapas in later chapters. It can also be served on its own, in little dishes, for drizzling over bread or for dipping bread into, alongside other tapas dishes.

PREPARATION TIME: 5 minutes

SERVES: 6

4 tablespoons extra virgin olive oil

1 tablespoon sherry vinegar

several sprigs of herbs, such as parsley, thyme, rosemary, oregano, chives and fennel

salt and pepper

1 Put the oil, vinegar and salt and pepper in a bowl.

2 Discard any tough stalks from the herbs and finely chop the leaves. Whisk into the dressing with a fork. Cover and chill until needed.

Cabrales with honey and walnuts
The salty flavour of Cabrales cheese, or any other Spanish blue cheese, is delicious drizzled with runny honey on a slice of well-flavoured crusty bread.

PREPARATION TIME: 10 minutes

COOKING TIME: 2 minutes

SERVES: 12

12 thin slices of rustic crusty bread

2 tablespoons extra virgin olive oil

100 g (3½ oz) Cabrales cheese

25 g (1 oz) roughly chopped walnuts, lightly toasted

2 tablespoons clear honey

mild sweet paprika, to sprinkle (optional)

1 Lightly toast the bread on both sides and drizzle with the oil.

2 Discard any rind from the Cabrales and roughly crumble the cheese over the bread.

3 Scatter with the walnuts. Transfer to a serving plate, drizzle with the honey and sprinkle with paprika, if liked.

Variation Pecans, almonds or hazelnuts can be used instead of the walnuts.

Quails' eggs with herb salt

Delicate, creamy flavoured quails' eggs are the perfect size for dipping into this delicious salt. Rather than shelling all the eggs, leave some whole because they look so pretty, or, if you're pushed for time, let everyone shell their own.

PREPARATION TIME: 5 minutes

COOKING TIME: 2 minutes

SERVES: 5–6

24 quails' eggs, at room temperature

15 g (½ oz) coarse sea salt

2 teaspoons finely chopped rosemary

1 teaspoon finely chopped thyme

½ teaspoon freshly ground black pepper

1 Put the eggs in a small saucepan and cover with just-boiled water. Return to the boil and cook for 2 minutes. Drain the eggs, run them under the cold tap to cool, then shell them.

2 Mix the salt with the herbs and pepper.

3 To serve, put the salt in tiny dishes and serve on individual plates with the eggs for dipping.

Lettuce hearts with anchovy dressing

This is a lovely combination of fresh, cooling lettuce with a contrasting garlicky, salty dressing, and it's perfect with a glass of chilled white wine. Use small, crisp, hearty lettuces – Little Gems are ideal – or use a larger lettuce and cut it into small wedges.

PREPARATION TIME: 10 minutes

SERVES: 4–6

2 hearty Little Gem lettuces

1 garlic clove, chopped

50 g (2 oz) can anchovy fillets in olive oil

4 tablespoons chopped parsley

4 tablespoons extra virgin olive oil

1 tablespoon white wine vinegar

pepper

1 Cut each lettuce into 6 wedges and arrange them in a shallow dish or several small dishes.

2 Put the garlic, anchovy fillets and their oil, parsley, oil, vinegar and pepper in a food processor and blend to make a fairly smooth dressing.

3 Spoon the dressing over the lettuce wedges and serve immediately.

Marinated anchovies

Marinating fish in vinegar prolongs the storage life for up to a week in the refrigerator. This recipe, which is served in tapas bars all over Spain, makes an appetizing little snack with some olives and bread for mopping up the juices.

PREPARATION TIME: 20 minutes, plus marinating

SERVES: 4

250 g (8 oz) fresh anchovies

100 ml (3½ fl oz) white wine vinegar

2 garlic cloves, crushed

2 tablespoons finely chopped parsley

100 ml (3½ fl oz) olive oil

salt and pepper

1 Cut off the fish heads, slit open the undersides and gut the fish. Pull away the backbones and rinse the fish under cold running water.

2 Arrange the anchovies in a non-metallic dish and cover with the vinegar. Cover and chill overnight.

3 Mix together the garlic, parsley, oil and salt and pepper.

4 Drain the vinegar from the anchovies and add the garlic mixture. Cover and chill for several hours or overnight before serving.

Tip If you're unable to get fresh anchovies, you can try this recipe with very small sardines. The fish must be absolutely fresh when you pickle them, then they'll keep in the refrigerator for days.

Griddled vegetables

Griddling Mediterranean vegetables brings out their ripe, juicy flavours, and just a few slices, served with a little pot of Aïoli (see page 34) or Romesco Sauce (see page 35) makes a tasty dish. Other vegetables, such as thinly sliced fennel or peppers, can also be used.

PREPARATION TIME: 10 minutes

COOKING TIME: 20–25 minutes

SERVES: 6

1 aubergine, about 250 g (8 oz)

2 courgettes

18 asparagus spears

5 tablespoons olive oil

1 tablespoon finely chopped oregano

salt and pepper

1 Cut the aubergine lengthways into slices 1 cm (¹/₂ inch) thick. Slice the courgettes lengthways. Snap off the woody parts of the asparagus stems.

2 Heat a large, ridged griddle pan or heavy-based frying pan. Mix the oil with the oregano and salt and pepper and brush the mixture all over the vegetables.

3 Cook the vegetables in batches, starting with the aubergines, which will take about 15 minutes, turning them over halfway through cooking. Push the slices to one side or transfer them to a plate and cook the courgettes and asparagus, turning once, for 5–10 minutes until tender. Serve warm.

Tomato and garlic bread

Another well-loved and delicious tapas dish, this is known as pa amb tomaquet *in Catalonia. Its success relies on using the best tomatoes, olive oil and bread.*

PREPARATION TIME: 5 minutes

COOKING TIME: 2 minutes

SERVES: 4

4 small, very ripe tomatoes, skinned

4 thin slices of rustic white bread

1 garlic clove, halved

4 teaspoons extra virgin olive oil

4 slices of Serrano ham

pepper

1 Mash the tomatoes against the side of a bowl or finely chop them if they are slightly firmer.

2 Lightly toast the bread on both sides and rub it with the cut side of the garlic clove while the bread is still hot.

3 Pile the tomatoes on top and drizzle with the oil. Crumple the Serrano ham over the tomatoes and serve seasoned with black pepper.

Tip The Spanish squeeze the juicy pulp from the tomatoes over the bread, but if you've struggled to find well-flavoured tomatoes, you might not want to waste any.

Marinated olives *If you've bought quite ordinary olives and want to dress them up a bit, try steeping them in this blend of herbs and spices. They can be eaten after a couple of hours or stored in the refrigerator for up to a week.*

PREPARATION TIME: 10 minutes

MAKES: 250 g (8 oz)

250 g (8 oz) black or green olives

several pared strips of orange rind

4 bay leaves

1 small garlic clove, crushed

1 teaspoon cumin seeds

1 teaspoon coriander seeds

1 teaspoon fennel seeds

2 tablespoons finely chopped fresh coriander

2 tablespoons red, white or sherry vinegar

about 150 ml (¼ pint) olive oil

pepper

1 Put the olives in a bowl and scatter over the orange rind, bay leaves and garlic.

2 Crush all the seeds using a pestle and mortar and add them to the bowl with the coriander, vinegar and a little black pepper. Mix well and turn into a small bowl or jar into which they fit quite snugly – a 350 ml (12 fl oz) capacity wide-necked preserving jar is ideal – and pack them down with the back of a spoon.

3 Pour over the oil so the olives are just immersed, cover with a lid or foil and store in the refrigerator.

Aïoli *Raw garlic can give aïoli quite a harsh flavour, so in this recipe it's lightly roasted first. As a short cut, omit the roasting but halve the amount of garlic used.*

PREPARATION TIME: 10 minutes

COOKING TIME: 30 minutes

SERVES: 6

4 garlic cloves

2 egg yolks

200 ml (7 fl oz) olive oil

1 tablespoon white wine vinegar

salt and pepper

1 Roast the garlic by nestling it in a little foil and cooking in a preheated oven, 180°C (350°F), Gas Mark 4, for 30 minutes or until softened. (It's worth doing this when you've already got the oven on because the roasted cloves will keep overnight in the refrigerator.)

2 Push the garlic out of the skins into a food processor. Add the egg yolks and blend briefly to combine. With the machine running, slowly add the oil in a thin trickle until thickened. Stir in the vinegar and salt and pepper to taste and turn into a small bowl. Cover tightly and chill.

Tip If the aïoli separates during the process of adding the oil, tip it into a jug and add another egg yolk to the machine. Gradually add the separated mixture in a thin trickle.

Romesco sauce
This classic Spanish sauce is great with almost any vegetables as well as poultry, fish and shellfish. Serve it cold, in little dishes for spooning over or dipping. It's really good with Griddled Vegetables (see page 31), and you can keep leftovers, covered, in the refrigerator for several days.

PREPARATION TIME: 15 minutes, plus soaking

COOKING TIME: 10 minutes

SERVES: 8

15 g (½ oz) dried sweet peppers (see page 12)

1 dried red chilli, or fresh chilli, deseeded and chopped

100 g (3½ oz) blanched almonds

75 ml (3 fl oz) extra virgin olive oil

50 g (2 oz) sliced bread, diced

1 red pepper, deseeded and chopped

4 tomatoes, skinned and roughly chopped

2 garlic cloves, roughly chopped

1–2 tablespoons sherry vinegar

salt

1 Soak the dried peppers and dried chilli (if used) in boiling water for 30 minutes to soften. Lightly toast the nuts in a dry frying pan.

2 Thoroughly drain the peppers and roughly chop the flesh. Heat half the oil in a frying pan and gently cook the bread until golden. Drain. Add the red pepper and dried peppers, fresh chilli (if used), tomatoes and garlic and fry gently, stirring, for 5 minutes.

3 Grind the nuts in a food processor. Add the bread and blend to a paste. Add the tomato mixture and the remaining oil and blend again to make a thick sauce. Add the vinegar to taste, season with salt and turn into a serving dish. Cover and chill until ready to serve.

Cheese and egg *These recipes use cheese and eggs as the predominant flavours, although they might also be used in smaller amounts in recipes in later chapters. Apart from Manchego, Spanish cheeses are not particularly well known internationally, so take the opportunity to buy them when you can. Look out for creamy Tetilla, which can be served as it is but melts beautifully when cooked. Rich, blue-veined Cabrales is also worth seeking out, as are all the lesser known goats' and ewes' milk cheeses. This section includes a couple of recipes for tortilla, one of Spain's best-known dishes and a tapas classic. Try the basic potato tortilla or the slightly more elaborate version – both are delicious – but make sure that you use the best quality eggs you can find.*

Asparagus and green bean tortilla
This tortilla uses green beans and asparagus, but chopped peppers, broad beans, mushrooms, chorizo or morcilla all make good additions

PREPARATION TIME: 15 minutes

COOKING TIME: 30 minutes

SERVES: 8

150 g (5 oz) green beans, halved

300 g (10 oz) asparagus, trimmed

150 ml (¼ pint) light olive oil

1 medium potato, cut into 1 cm (½ inch) dice

1 medium leek, chopped

8 free-range, organic eggs

1 garlic clove, crushed

1 tablespoon chopped lemon thyme

3 tablespoons chopped parsley

salt and pepper

1 Blanch the beans in boiling water for 3 minutes and drain. Cut the asparagus into 5 cm (2 inch) lengths. Heat the oil in a sturdy, 24–25 cm (9½–10 inch), heavy-based frying pan with deep sides. Add the potato and fry gently for 5 minutes. Add the leek and fry for 5 minutes.

2 Add the asparagus, beans and salt and pepper and cook gently for 5 minutes or until the vegetables are tender. Tip into a sieve over a saucepan to catch the oil, so that most of the oil is drained off. Return the vegetables to the frying pan.

3 Beat the eggs in a bowl with a little salt and pepper. Pour over the vegetables. Reduce the heat to its lowest setting and cook for about 10 minutes or until the tortilla is still just a little soft in the centre.

4 Meanwhile, add the garlic and herbs to the drained oil and warm through.

5 Position a plate over the pan and invert the tortilla on to it. Slide it back into the pan and cook for a couple of minutes to set the base. Slide on to a serving plate and drizzle with the herb oil.

Potato tortilla *This is eaten virtually all over Spain, sometimes made simply with potatoes and onions or on other occasions with the addition of various vegetables (see page 38) or meats.*

PREPARATION TIME: 15 minutes

COOKING TIME: 35 minutes

SERVES: 8

150 ml (¼ pint) light olive oil

1 onion, chopped

750 g (1½ lb) medium waxy potatoes, thinly sliced

6 free-range, organic eggs

salt and pepper

1 Heat the oil in a sturdy, 24–25 cm (9½–10 inch), heavy-based frying pan with deep sides. Tip in the onion and potatoes and season with plenty of salt and pepper. Reduce the heat to its lowest setting and cook gently, turning frequently so the vegetables cook evenly, for 20–25 minutes. Don't use too high a temperature or the potatoes will start to catch before they're cooked through.

2 Thoroughly beat the eggs in a bowl with a little more salt and pepper. Drain the potatoes and onions, reserving the oil.

3 Wipe out the pan and heat 3 tablespoons of the reserved oil. Tip in the vegetables and spread them out into an even layer.

4 Pour over the egg mixture, reduce the heat to its lowest setting and cook gently for about 10 minutes until the tortilla is still a little soft in the centre.

5 Position a large plate over the pan and quickly invert the tortilla on to it. Carefully slide it back into the pan and cook for a further couple of minutes to set the base. Slide on to a serving plate and serve warm or cold.

Soft cheese and fennel salad
A mixture of crisp shredded vegetables makes a well-flavoured, refreshing salad that's perfect for accompanying meatier tapas dishes.

PREPARATION TIME: 15 minutes, plus standing

SERVES: 8–10

1 cucumber, peeled and thickly sliced

3 tablespoons salt

1 large fennel bulb, about 300 g (10 oz), cut into wedges

100 g (3½ oz) sugarsnap peas

1 small red onion, roughly chopped

50 g (2 oz) small, pitted black or green olives

100 g (3½ oz) goats' cheese, cut into small dice

2 teaspoons fennel seeds, lightly crushed

4 tablespoons extra virgin olive oil

pepper

1 Layer the cucumber slices in a colander, sprinkling each layer with salt. Leave to stand for 20 minutes.

2 Thoroughly rinse the cucumber in plenty of cold water to remove all traces of salt.

3 Put the cucumber slices, fennel, sugarsnaps and onion through a food processor fitted with a fine slicer attachment. Tip the vegetables into a bowl and stir in the olives and cheese.

4 Heat the fennel seeds in a small saucepan for a couple of minutes to toast lightly. Tip into a bowl and mix in the oil and plenty of pepper. Toss the dressing with the salad and chill until ready to serve.

Coco with spinach and goats' cheese

A coco is very much like a pizza and similarly can be topped with various ingredients. This one uses spinach, goats' cheese, pine nuts and mushrooms.

PREPARATION TIME: 30 minutes, plus proving

COOKING TIME: 25 minutes

MAKES: 12 small squares

200 g (7 oz) strong plain flour

¼ teaspoon salt

1 teaspoon easy-blend dried yeast

50 ml (2 fl oz) olive oil, plus 2 tablespoons

125 g (4 oz) mushrooms, thinly sliced

4 garlic cloves, thinly sliced

50 g (2 oz) pine nuts

225 g (7½ oz) young spinach leaves

½ teaspoon mild sweet or smoked paprika, plus extra to sprinkle

150 g (5 oz) soft goats' cheese

salt

1 Make the bread base. Put the flour, salt and yeast in a bowl with 50 ml (2 fl oz) oil. Add 100 ml (3½ fl oz) hand-hot water and mix to a soft dough, adding a little more water if the mixture feels dry. Turn out on to a floured surface and knead for 10 minutes until smooth and elastic. Put it in a lightly oiled bowl, cover with clingfilm and leave to rise until doubled in size (about 45 minutes).

2 Oil a baking sheet. Punch the dough to deflate and turn it out on to a floured surface. Roll it out to a 25 cm (10 inch) square and transfer to the baking sheet.

3 Heat 2 tablespoons oil in a frying pan and gently fry the mushrooms, garlic and pine nuts for 3 minutes. Add the spinach and cook until wilted. Sprinkle with the paprika and a little salt.

4 Turn the mixture on to the base, spreading it in an even layer. Dot the cheese over the spinach. Sprinkle with extra paprika and bake in a preheated oven, 200°C (400°F), Gas Mark 6, for 20 minutes until golden.

Coco with spinach and goats' cheese

Potted Cabrales
Mature Cabrales has a strong flavour, which can be softened by mixing it with a light, creamy cheese. If you can't get Cabrales, try another blue-veined Spanish cheese or a Stilton or Roquefort.

PREPARATION TIME: 10 minutes, plus chilling

SERVES: 10

65 g (2½ oz) butter

plenty of freshly grated nutmeg

250 g (8 oz) ricotta cheese

125 g (4 oz) Cabrales cheese

2 tablespoons chopped chives,
**   plus extra whole chives to garnish**

thin slices of seeded or walnut bread, toasted

pepper

1 Melt the butter with the nutmeg. Press the ricotta cheese through a sieve into a bowl. Cut any rind from the Cabrales and crumble it into the bowl. Stir in about two-thirds of the butter, the chives and plenty of pepper until evenly mixed.

2 Pack the mixture into a 450 ml (³/4 pint) shallow dish and spread it level with the back of a spoon.

3 Drizzle with the remaining butter and chill for at least 2 hours, or until ready to serve.

4 Spoon the cheese on to the toast and serve garnished with extra chives.

Tip The cheese can also be potted in tiny dishes, not much bigger than butter dishes, for serving individual portions with bread or toast.

Pepper and tomato frito with quails' eggs

Cooking peppers slowly and gently brings out their deliciously sweet Mediterranean flavour. Any leftover mixture reheats well and makes a good filling for toasted sandwiches with melting cheese.

PREPARATION TIME: 15 minutes

COOKING TIME: 30 minutes

SERVES: 8

3 red peppers, cored and deseeded

4 tablespoons olive oil

1 red onion, thinly sliced

2 garlic cloves, thinly sliced

400 g (13 oz) tomatoes,
    skinned and roughly chopped

2 tablespoons sun-dried tomato paste

1 tablespoon chopped sage

1 tablespoon capers, rinsed and drained

8 quails' eggs

salt and pepper

1 Slice the peppers as thinly as possible. (This is best done using the slicer attachment of a food processor.)

2 Heat 2 tablespoons of the oil in a large saucepan or frying pan and fry the onion for 5 minutes until softened. Add the peppers and fry for a further 10 minutes or until beginning to brown.

3 Add the garlic, tomatoes, tomato paste, sage and capers and cover with a lid. Cook very gently, stirring occasionally, for about 10 minutes until the mixture is soft and pulpy.

4 Heat another tablespoon of the oil in a small frying pan. Break the eggs into the pan and fry gently until set.

5 Stir the remaining oil into the pepper mixture, season to taste with salt and pepper and spoon into small, warmed dishes. Slide a fried egg on top of each dish to serve.

Grilled goats' cheese with piquillo salsa

Use a firm but full-flavoured goats' cheese with rind so it holds its shape during grilling. If you can't get a jar of peppers used roasted ones, either your own or those available from most deli counters.

PREPARATION TIME: 10 minutes

COOKING TIME: 3–5 minutes

MAKES: 10

oil, for brushing

1 tablespoon finely chopped rosemary

½ teaspoon freshly ground red or black pepper

150 g (5 oz) cylindrical piece goats' cheese, about 5 cm (2 inches) across

a little beaten egg white

Salsa

100 g (3½ oz) piquillo peppers from a jar, drained

1 spring onion, finely chopped

finely grated rind of 1 lime, plus 1 tablespoon juice

2 teaspoons caster sugar

1 Make the salsa. Slice the peppers as thinly as possible and mix them in a bowl with the spring onion, lime juice and sugar.

2 Lightly brush a foil-lined grill rack with oil. Mix the rosemary with the ground pepper.

3 Coat the rind of the cheese in egg white and roll it in the rosemary and pepper mixture. Cut the cheese across into 10 slices 1 cm (¹/₂ inch) thick and place them on the foil.

4 Cook under a preheated grill until the cheese starts to bubble and turn brown. Slide on to small plates and top each with a small spoonful of the salsa. Drizzle any juices on to the plates and top the salsa with the lime rind.

Bunuelos

These little fritters can be flavoured with meat, fish, herbs or, as in this case, with Manchego cheese, and they make perfect little bite-sized appetizers. Make and shape them in advance to cut down last-minute preparation.

PREPARATION TIME: 20 minutes

COOKING TIME: 15 minutes

MAKES: 28

75 g (3 oz) flaked almonds or pine nuts

75 g (3 oz) plain flour

100 ml (3½ fl oz) milk

1 egg and 1 yolk

150 g (5 oz) Manchego cheese, finely grated

mild olive oil or sunflower oil, for deep-frying

salt and pepper

1 Use your fingers to break the almonds into smaller pieces or roughly chop the pine nuts. Scatter them on a plate.

2 Sift the flour on to a piece of greaseproof paper. Bring the milk to the boil in a saucepan with 100 ml (3½ fl oz) water. Remove from the heat and tip in the flour. Beat with a wooden spoon until the dough forms a smooth, thick paste. Leave to cool slightly.

3 Beat the egg with the extra yolk and gradually mix into the dough. Stir in all but 2 tablespoons of the cheese and a little salt and pepper.

4 Take teaspoonfuls of the mixture, drop them on to the plate of nuts and turn them lightly in the nuts so they're roughly coated. Finish by rolling them lightly into balls.

5 Heat the oil to a depth of 5 cm (2 inches) in a large saucepan or deep-fat fryer until a little of the dough sizzles on the surface. Cook the fritters in batches for about 3 minutes until they are golden. Drain on kitchen paper and serve sprinkled with the reserved cheese.

Empanadas

Both ingredients and method for these tiny little pastries vary enormously throughout Spain. Some cooks use pastry, others bread dough, and there is an equally diverse range of fillings.

PREPARATION TIME: 30 minutes, plus chilling

COOKING TIME: 20 minutes

MAKES: 16

250 g (8 oz) plain flour

175 g (6 oz) lightly salted butter, cut into small dice

2 egg yolks

sea salt and pepper

Filling

25 g (1 oz) basil

50 g (2 oz) pitted green olives

150 g (5 oz) Manchego cheese, grated

1 Put the flour and butter in a food processor and blend until the mixture resembles fine breadcrumbs. Add 1 egg yolk and 1 tablespoon cold water and mix to a dough. Knead lightly to make a smooth dough, cover and chill for at least 30 minutes.

2 Make the filling. Put the basil and olives in a food processor and blend briefly until both basil and olives are finely chopped. Mix them in a bowl with the cheese and plenty of black pepper.

3 Grease 2 baking sheets. Thinly roll out the pastry on a floured surface and cut out rounds with an 8–9 cm (3¼–3¾ inch) pastry cutter or upturned bowl.

4 Mix the second egg yolk with 1 teaspoon water and lightly brush the edges of the pastry. Spoon the filling into the centres. Bring the pastry edges together over the filling, press them firmly together and crimp with your fingertips.

5 Place the empanadas on the baking sheets and brush with the remaining egg yolk, sprinkle with sea salt and bake in a preheated oven, 190°C (375°F), Gas Mark 5, for 20 minutes.

Spiced cheese and pear melts

Use very ripe, juicy pears for this recipe so they make a prefect flavour contrast to the spicy saltiness of the cheese. Many pears are underripe when bought, so leave them in the fruit bowl for a few days to ripen.

PREPARATION TIME: 10 minutes

COOKING TIME: 5 minutes

MAKES: 8

10 cardamom pods

1 teaspoon mustard seeds

½ teaspoon cumin seeds

½ teaspoon sea salt

8 slices of bread 5 mm (¼ inch) thick and 5–7 cm (2–3 inches) across

1 tablespoon chopped raisins

150 g (5 oz) buffalo mozzarella, cut into 8 slices

1 small, juicy pear

1 tablespoon chilli-infused oil

1 Crush the cardamom pods using a pestle and mortar, then scoop out the pieces of shell. Add the mustard seeds and cumin seeds and crush until fairly finely ground. Stir in the salt.

2 Line a grill rack with foil and lightly toast the bread on one side. Turn the slices over and scatter with the raisins and a sprinkling of the spice mix.

3 Lay the mozzarella slices over the bread and sprinkle with the remaining spice mix. Cut the pear into 8 wedges, discarding the core, and place the wedges over the cheese. Drizzle with 2 teaspoons oil.

4 Cook under a preheated grill for 2–3 minutes until hot. Transfer to small plates and drizzle with the remaining oil.

Cheese, ham and garlic toasts

Use a small, rounded loaf for this recipe so that each sandwich can be cut into two finger-sized portions. Tetilla is a good cooking cheese as it melts so well, but Cheddar or Emmental can be used instead.

PREPARATION TIME: 10 minutes

COOKING TIME: 5 minutes

SERVES: 6

65 g (2½ oz) butter, softened

2 garlic cloves, crushed

good pinch of hot smoked paprika

12 thin slices from a small crusty loaf

50 g (2 oz) lomo or Serrano ham, sliced wafer thin

75 g (3 oz) Tetilla or Manchego cheese, thinly sliced

salt

1 Beat the butter in a bowl with the garlic, paprika and a little salt until well mixed.

2 Use half the spiced butter to spread one side of each bread. Sandwich the slices together with the ham and cheese.

3 Butter the outsides of the bread slices with the remaining spiced butter.

4 Heat a large, heavy-based frying pan or griddle and gently fry the sandwiches, in batches if necessary, for 2–3 minutes on each side until golden. Cut the slices in half to serve.

Meat, poultry and game

Meaty tapas dishes can be reasonably light and appetizing — see the Roasted Stuffed Tomatoes on page 70, for example — or more seriously hearty, like meatballs or braised lamb. These are the sort of dishes you would serve as part of a complete tapas meal because you certainly wouldn't want to go on to eat a main course. Pork, poultry and small game feature highly in this section as they do generally in Spanish cuisine. The distinctive flavours of chorizo, morcilla, paprika and other spices crop up several times, adding plenty of colour and flavour. Prepare as much in advance as you can, particularly the stews, which can be made ahead and reheated so that you can relax and enjoy them too. By this stage of the meal you might be ready to serve some heartier, full-bodied Spanish red wines.

Meatballs in tomato sauce
There are many different recipes for tapas-style meatballs. Adding anchovies enhances the flavour of the meat, but they are not essential if you prefer to leave them out.

PREPARATION TIME: 25 minutes

COOKING TIME: 45 minutes

SERVES: 8–10

400 g (13 oz) lean minced beef

300 g (10 oz) minced pork

6 canned anchovy fillets, drained and chopped

25 g (1 oz) breadcrumbs

3 garlic cloves, chopped

6 tablespoons olive oil

1 large onion, chopped

1 kg (2 lb) tomatoes, skinned and chopped

150 ml (¼ pint) white wine

3 bay leaves

3 tablespoons sun-dried tomato paste

2 teaspoons mild sweet paprika

salt and pepper

1 Put the beef, pork, anchovies, breadcrumbs, garlic and salt and pepper in a food processor and mix to form a smooth, thick paste. (Alternatively, mix in a bowl with your hands.) Shape the mixture into small balls, about 3 cm (1¹/4 inches) across.

2 Heat 3 tablespoons of oil in a large frying pan and gently fry the meatballs, shaking the pan frequently, for about 10 minutes until they are browned all over. Remove the meatballs with a slotted spoon.

3 Add the onion to the pan and fry gently until softened. Stir in the tomatoes, wine, bay leaves, tomato paste, paprika, the remaining oil and a little salt and pepper. Bring to the boil, reduce the heat and simmer gently for about 20 minutes until thick and pulpy.

4 Tip the meatballs into the pan and heat through gently for 5 minutes.

Tip This is a good 'make ahead' dish that reheats well.

Lamb cutlets with mojo sauce

Small, lean lamb cutlets, with bone intact for a natural handle, make impressive finger food. Get ahead by trimming off the fat and making the sauce in advance.

PREPARATION TIME: 10 minutes

COOKING TIME: 10 minutes

SERVES: 8

8 small lamb cutlets

1 garlic clove, crushed

1 tablespoon chopped thyme

3 tablespoons olive oil

salt and pepper

Sauce

2 medium-strength red chillies, deseeded and chopped

4 garlic cloves, roughly chopped

2 teaspoons cumin seeds, crushed

small handful of fresh coriander

4 tablespoons olive oil

1 tablespoon sherry vinegar

1 Trim the lamb cutlets of most of the fat, scraping it away completely from the tips of the bones.

2 Mix together the garlic, thyme, oil and a little salt and pepper and spread over the lamb.

3 Make the sauce. Put the chillies, garlic, cumin seeds, coriander and oil in a food processor and blend to a thin paste. Stir in the vinegar, season with a little salt and turn into a small dish.

4 Heat a griddle or heavy-based frying pan and fry the lamb for about 4 minutes on each side. (The cooking time will vary depending on the thickness of the cutlets. This length of time should leave 2.5 cm/1 inch thick cutlets slightly pink in the centre, so cook them for longer if you prefer them cooked through.) Serve the sauce with a small spoon for drizzling it over the cutlets.

Tip Any leftover sauce is delicious with grilled meats, or fish or vegetable stews.

Braised lamb with chickpeas and saffron

Lamb tenderloin is good for this recipe because it comes in conveniently small pieces, but any other lean, boneless lamb can be used instead.

PREPARATION TIME: 15 minutes

COOKING TIME: 1 1/2 hours

SERVES: 6–8

500 g (1 lb) lean lamb fillet

2 tablespoons olive oil

1 onion, finely chopped

3 garlic cloves, crushed

100 ml (3½ fl oz) medium sherry

150 ml (¼ pint) chicken or lamb stock

1 teaspoon saffron strands

400 g (13 oz) can chickpeas, drained

salt and pepper

1 Trim any excess fat from the lamb and cut the meat into small chunks. Season with salt and pepper.

2 Heat the oil in a frying pan and fry the lamb in 2 batches until it is beginning to colour. Transfer it with a slotted spoon to a small ovenproof dish.

3 Add the onion and garlic to the frying pan and fry gently for 3 minutes. Add the sherry and stock and crumble in the saffron. Bring the sauce to the boil then pour it over the lamb. Cover with a lid and bake in a preheated oven, 160°C (325°F), Gas Mark 3, for 1 hour or until the lamb is tender.

4 Stir in the chickpeas and return the dish to the oven for 15 minutes. Check the seasoning and serve hot.

Pork with tomatoes and olives

Dried tomatoes give a wonderful burst of Mediterranean flavour to this simple dish. Lamb or beef is also delicious instead of the pork if you prefer.

PREPARATION TIME: 15 minutes, plus soaking

COOKING TIME: 1¹/4 hours

SERVES: 8

100 g (3½ oz) dried tomatoes

500 g (1 lb) pork fillet or leg of pork

2 teaspoons crushed fennel seeds

2 tablespoons olive oil

1 onion, chopped

150 ml (¼ pint) white wine

400 g (13 oz) can chopped tomatoes

40 g (1½ oz) pitted black olives, chopped

1 tablespoon chopped oregano

1 tablespoon capers, rinsed

salt and pepper

1 Put the dried tomatoes in a bowl, cover with boiling water and leave to soak for 30 minutes until softened.

2 Cut the pork into small chunks, discarding any excess fat. Mix the fennel seeds with a little salt and pepper and use the mixture to coat the pork.

3 Heat the oil in a frying pan and fry the pork in 2 batches until browned. Transfer to an ovenproof dish with a slotted spoon. Add the onion to the frying pan and fry for 5 minutes. Add the wine and boil until reduced by about half. Tip the mixture over the pork.

4 Drain the dried tomatoes and blend in a food processor with the canned tomatoes, olives, oregano and capers. Add the mixture to the dish.

5 Cover with a lid and cook in a preheated oven, 160°C (325°F), Gas Mark 3, for about 1 hour or until the pork is tender. Check the seasoning and serve in small, warmed dishes.

Moorish pork pinchitos

A pincho is a small stick, and in tapas terms the word refers to the small skewers on which ingredients are often threaded, making them easier to eat.

PREPARATION TIME: 20 minutes, plus marinating
COOKING TIME: 12 minutes
SERVES: 14–16

300 g (10 oz) piece skinless pork loin

2 teaspoons lightly crushed cumin seeds

¼ teaspoon cayenne pepper

good pinch of ground cinnamon

1 pickled lemon, about 20 g (¾ oz)

2 garlic cloves, crushed

3 tablespoons finely chopped parsley

4 tablespoons olive oil

salt and pepper

1 Trim any fat from the pork and cut the meat into thin slices. Mix together the cumin seeds, cayenne, cinnamon and salt and pepper and rub the mixture over both sides of the pork slices. Leave to marinate for at least 15 minutes.

2 Halve the lemon and scoop out and discard the pulpy centres. Finely chop the rest and mix with the garlic and parsley in a bowl.

3 Heat a large, heavy-based frying pan or griddle until very hot. Brush one side of the pork slices with oil and fry, oiled sides down, for 3 minutes. Brush the upper sides with more oil, turn the slices and cook for a further 3 minutes or until cooked through.

4 Thread the meat on to small wooden or metal skewers, one piece per skewer, and serve sprinkled with the lemon mixture.

Fabada Asturiana
This Asturian bean dish, cooked long and slow, is usually served as a main course, but it also makes a good wintry dish for tapas. Rather like the French cassoulet, it's a blend of rich, meaty flavours in a thick, tender bean stew.

PREPARATION TIME: 15 minutes, plus soaking

COOKING TIME: 2¹/₂ hours

SERVES: 8

300 g (10 oz) butter beans, soaked overnight

4 tablespoons olive oil

100 g (3½ oz) smoked bacon lardons

300 g (10 oz) lean belly pork, skinned and cut into large pieces

1 onion, chopped

100 g (3½ oz) hot or mild chorizo, cut into small pieces

100 g (3½ oz) morcilla, cut into small pieces

15 g (½ oz) dried red peppers, broken into pieces

good pinch of saffron threads

salt and pepper

1 Drain the beans, put them in a saucepan and cover with plenty of cold water. Bring to the boil and boil for 20 minutes until they are just beginning to soften. Drain and tip into a casserole dish.

2 Heat 2 tablespoons of the oil in a frying pan and fry the bacon lardons, belly pork and onion until lightly browned.

3 Add the contents of the frying pan to the casserole dish with the chorizo, morcilla and peppers. Crumble in the saffron threads and pour over just enough cold water to cover the ingredients.

4 Cover the casserole with a lid and bake in a preheated oven, 180°C (350°F), Gas Mark 4, for about 2 hours or until the beans are tender and the juices have thickened slightly.

Smoked pork and chorizo sausages

The spicy, salty flavour of these tiny sausages is great with the sweetness of the accompanying onion chutney. As a short cut you could use any ready-made onion or fruity chutney.

PREPARATION TIME: 30 minutes

COOKING TIME: 25 minutes

MAKES: 35–40

450 g (14½ oz) lean pork shoulder

125 g (4 oz) chorizo

½ teaspoon hot smoked paprika

2 tablespoons sun-dried tomato paste

50 g (2 oz) breadcrumbs

175 g (6 oz) thin cut rashers of smoked
   streaky bacon

salt and pepper

Sauce

2 tablespoons olive oil

3 onions, chopped

200 ml (7 fl oz) medium sherry

2 tablespoons clear honey

1 Trim any skin and large areas of fat from the pork shoulder and cut the meat into small dice. Roughly dice the chorizo. Blend the meats, in batches, in a food processor, then turn the mixture into a bowl and add the paprika, tomato paste, breadcrumbs and a little salt.

2 Mix well (this is most easily done with your hands). Take teaspoonfuls of the mixture and shape it roughly into tiny sausages.

3 Cut each bacon rasher into 3 (or in half if they're short) and roll each sausage in a piece of bacon. Place in a roasting tin and cook in a preheated oven, 180°C (350°F), Gas Mark 4, for 25 minutes until deep golden and cooked through.

4 Meanwhile, make the sauce. Heat the oil in a frying pan, add the onions and fry gently for 15 minutes until they are deep golden and beginning to caramelize. Add the sherry and bring to the boil. Let the mixture bubble until thickened, then remove the pan from the heat and stir in the honey. Season with plenty of pepper and serve with the sausages.

Basil and pancetta croquettes

The best croquettes have a crisp, crunchy shell encasing a melting centre. They're a little fiddly to make but can be prepared ahead ready for last-minute frying.

PREPARATION TIME: 30 minutes, plus chilling

COOKING TIME: 20 minutes

MAKES: 24

50 g (2 oz) butter

1 small onion, finely chopped

1 red or orange pepper, cored, deseeded and finely chopped

100 g (3½ oz) pancetta, finely chopped

40 g (1½ oz) plain flour, plus extra to dust

300 ml (½ pint) milk

150 g (5 oz) Tetilla cheese, grated

15g (½ oz) basil leaves, shredded

2 eggs, beaten

125 g (4 oz) white breadcrumbs

sunflower oil, for deep-frying

salt and pepper

1 Line an 18 cm (7 inch) square, shallow dish with baking parchment. Melt the butter in a large frying pan and gently fry the onion, pepper and pancetta for 10 minutes until just starting to brown.

2 Add the flour and cook, stirring, for 1 minute. Gradually blend in the milk to make a smooth sauce. Boil for 2 minutes, stirring, until very thick. Stir in the cheese, basil and salt and pepper.

3 Turn the mixture into the lined tin, spreading it evenly. Cool, then chill for several hours or overnight until firm.

4 Turn out the mixture on to a board, peel away the paper and cut it into 24 pieces. Dust in flour, then dip each in the beaten egg and cover thickly in breadcrumbs.

5 Heat oil to a depth of 5 cm (2 inches) in a large, heavy-based saucepan or deep-fat fryer until a sprinkling of breadcrumbs sizzles on the surface. Fry the croquettes, in batches, until golden. Drain on kitchen paper while frying the remainder.

Basil and pancetta croquettes

Chorizo with new potatoes
Chorizo sausage is used in generous amounts in many tapas dishes, its spicy flavour infusing all the ingredients it's cooked with. Use a mild or spicier flavoured one, depending on personal taste.

PREPARATION TIME: 10 minutes

COOKING TIME: 25 minutes

SERVES: 8

550 g (1 lb 2 oz) new potatoes, cut into 2 cm (¾ inch) chunks

300 g (10 oz) chorizo

4 tablespoons olive oil

100 ml (3½ fl oz) dry sherry

salt and pepper

1 Cook the potatoes in lightly salted boiling water for 5 minutes until slightly softened. Drain.

2 Cut the chorizo into 2 cm ($^3/_4$ inch) chunks. Heat 2 tablespoons of the oil in a large frying pan. Add the potatoes and fry gently, stirring frequently, for 8–10 minutes until they are just beginning to turn golden. Remove the potatoes with a slotted spoon.

3 Add the remaining oil and the chorizo to the pan and fry for 5 minutes until lightly browned. Remove the pan from the heat and stir in the sherry. Cook gently, stirring frequently, until the sherry has mostly evaporated.

4 Return the potatoes to the pan, check the seasoning and heat through for 2 minutes before serving.

Cheese and chorizo puffs
These light, airy pastries can be made ahead and assembled on baking sheets, so you can pop them in the oven shortly before serving.

PREPARATION TIME: 30 minutes

COOKING TIME: 25 minutes

MAKES: 18–20

100 g (3½ oz) **soft chorizo**

2 tablespoons **sun-dried tomato paste**

1 tablespoon **chopped oregano**

3 tablespoons **olive oil**

100 g (3½ oz) **plain flour**

2 **eggs and 2 yolks**

50 g (2 oz) **ground almonds**

50 g (2 oz) **Manchego cheese, grated**

salt and pepper

1 Grease 2 baking sheets. Mash the chorizo in a bowl with the tomato paste and oregano. (If the sausage is quite firm, chop it into a food processor, add the tomato paste and oregano and blend to a paste.)

2 Bring 200 ml (7 fl oz) water to the boil in a saucepan with the oil then remove it from the heat. Tip in the flour, all in one go, and beat with a wooden spoon until smooth. Return to the heat and cook, beating with the spoon, until the mixture forms a stiff paste. Leave to cool for 2 minutes.

3 Beat the eggs with the yolks and gradually beat into the paste until smooth. Stir in the ground almonds, Manchego and a little salt and pepper.

4 Take dessertspoonfuls of the mixture and roll into balls. (Wetting the palms of your hands will stop the mixture from sticking.) Space them slightly apart on the baking sheets, flattening the rounds and making a hole in the centre. Spoon the chorizo mixture into the centres and bake in a preheated oven, 200°C (400°F), Gas Mark 6, for 20–25 minutes until risen and golden. Serve warm.

Morcilla with broad beans

With slow, gentle cooking, all the flavours in the morcilla sausage seep into the oil, making a delicious sauce for mopping up with bread. A spicy chorizo can be used instead.

PREPARATION TIME: 25 minutes

COOKING TIME: 25 minutes

SERVES: 6

300 g (10 oz) broad beans

200 g (7 oz) morcilla

100 ml (3½ fl oz) olive oil

1 small red onion, chopped

1 garlic clove, crushed

finely grated rind of 1 lemon,
    plus 1 tablespoon juice

3 tablespoons chopped parsley

salt and pepper

1 Cook the beans in boiling water for 3–5 minutes until tender. Drain and rinse under cold water.

2 Pop the beans out of their skins by pinching them between your thumb and finger. (Skinning the beans isn't essential but is worth doing if you have time as it reveals their fabulous colour and helps them absorb flavour.)

3 Roughly cut the morcilla into 1 cm (¹/2 inch) pieces, discarding the skin. Heat the oil in a frying pan, add the onion and morcilla and fry gently, stirring frequently, for 15 minutes or until the sausage is broken down.

4 Add the beans, garlic, lemon rind and juice and parsley to the pan and cook for 2–3 minutes until heated through. Season with salt and pepper and serve warm.

Morcilla with broad beans

Roasted stuffed tomatoes
These can be made well ahead and put in a dish so they're all ready for popping in the oven shortly before serving. Use a mild or spicy chorizo, whichever you prefer.

PREPARATION TIME: 30 minutes

COOKING TIME: 45 minutes

MAKES: 15

50 g (2 oz) short grain rice

50 g (2 oz) bulgar wheat

5 tablespoons olive oil

1 small onion, chopped

2 garlic cloves, chopped

2 teaspoons mild sweet paprika

125 g (4 oz) chorizo, chopped

2 teaspoons chopped lemon thyme,
  plus extra to sprinkle

15 medium tomatoes

salt and pepper

1 Cook the rice in plenty of boiling water for about 12 minutes or until tender. Put the bulgar wheat in a heatproof bowl, cover with 75 ml (3½ fl oz) boiling water and leave to stand for 10 minutes. Drain the rice and set aside.

2 Heat 2 tablespoons of oil in a pan, add the onion and fry gently for 5 minutes. Add the garlic, paprika, chorizo and thyme and fry gently for 2 minutes. Stir in the rice, bulgar wheat, another 2 tablespoons oil and salt and pepper.

3 Take a thin slice off the top of each tomato and scoop out the centres with a teaspoon.

4 Pack the stuffing mixture into the tomatoes and arrange them in a small ovenproof dish or roasting tin into which they fit quite snugly.

5 Drizzle the tomatoes with the remaining oil and plenty of black pepper and cook in a preheated oven, 190°C (375°F), Gas Mark 5, for 25 minutes until they are beginning to colour. Serve warm or cold, scattered with extra thyme.

Chorizo, fennel and potato soup

A flavoursome ham stock is ideal for this soup or, failing that, use a rich chicken stock. Serve in little bowls or small cups — espresso coffee cups are ideal.

PREPARATION TIME: 15 minutes

COOKING TIME: 30 minutes

SERVES: 8–10

3 tablespoons olive oil

1 onion, chopped

400 g (13 oz) fennel bulb, chopped

150 g (5 oz) chorizo, cut into small pieces

500 g (1 lb) floury potatoes, cut into small dice

1 litre (1¾ pints) meat stock

3 tablespoons finely chopped fresh coriander

3 tablespoons crème fraîche

salt and pepper

1 Heat the oil in a large saucepan and gently fry the onion and fennel for about 10 minutes until they are very soft and beginning to brown.

2 Add the chorizo, potatoes and stock and bring to the boil. Reduce the heat, cover with a lid and cook gently for 20 minutes until the potatoes are very tender.

3 Using a stick blender, blend the soup until fairly smooth. (Alternatively, blend briefly in a food processor.) Stir in the coriander and crème fraîche and heat through gently for a couple of minutes.

4 Season to taste and serve in small, warmed cups.

Chicken livers with Marsala and raisins

Use really fresh chicken livers so they're plump and creamy in their contrastingly sweet, syrupy sauce. Serve in little dishes or on slices of olive oil-drizzled toast. Accompany them with a glass of full-bodied sherry or red wine.

PREPARATION TIME: 10 minutes

COOKING TIME: about 10 minutes

SERVES: 5–6

400 g (13 oz) fresh chicken livers

25 g (1 oz) butter

2 tablespoons olive oil

25 g (1 oz) raisins

6 tablespoons Marsala

squeeze of lemon juice

salt and pepper

plenty of chopped chives, to garnish

1 Rinse the livers and pat them dry on kitchen paper. Cut each into about 4 pieces, cutting out and discarding any white parts. Season with salt and pepper.

2 Melt the butter with the oil in a frying pan. When it is very hot, add the livers and fry them quickly, turning them so they brown evenly, for 5 minutes until golden. If you prefer the livers well done, fry them for a couple of minutes longer. Add the raisins and fry for 1 minute.

3 Remove the livers and raisins with a slotted spoon and keep them warm.

4 Add the Marsala to the pan and bring to the boil. Cook for a couple of minutes until syrupy. Add the lemon juice then pour the sauce over the livers. Serve scattered with chives.

Spiced chicken wings

Like any succulent meat served on the bone, these sweet, spicy chicken wings are delicious but slightly messy to eat – not the best choice for a smart gathering. For a hotter flavour, add a dash of cayenne to the glaze.

PREPARATION TIME: 15 minutes

COOKING TIME: 1–1¹/₄ hours

SERVES: 6

1 kg (2 lb) chicken wings

3 tablespoons clear honey

1 tablespoon mild sweet paprika

4 garlic cloves, crushed

3 tablespoons olive oil

1 tablespoon wine vinegar

salt and pepper

chopped parsley, to garnish

1 Cut off the chicken wing tips then halve each wing through the joint using a sharp knife or poultry shears. Place the wings in a roasting tin. Put the honey in a small bowl with the paprika, garlic, oil, vinegar and a little salt and pepper. Mix well together.

2 Spoon the mixture over the chicken so the pieces are completely coated.

3 Cook the wings in a preheated oven, 180°C (350°F), Gas Mark 4, for 1–1¹/₄ hours, basting them frequently with the juices, until the chicken wings are deep golden and tender.

4 Spoon the wings into small dishes and drizzle with any remaining cooking juices. Scatter with parsley and serve.

Duck with saffron and pine nuts
This delicious combination of flavours is not traditionally served as tapas but more often as a main course. Served in very small portions, however, it does make a fabulous little 'taster' dish.

PREPARATION TIME: 15 minutes

COOKING TIME: 25 minutes

SERVES: 6

2 large duck breasts

¼ teaspoon ground cinnamon

½ teaspoon caster sugar

1 tablespoon olive oil

1 shallot, finely chopped

150 ml (¼ pint) white wine

2 garlic cloves, crushed

½ teaspoon saffron threads

25 g (1 oz) pine nuts

20 g (¾ oz) raisins

1 tablespoon medium sherry

salt and pepper

1 Trim any excess areas of fat from the duck. Mix together the cinnamon, sugar and salt and pepper and rub the mixture over the duck.

2 Heat the oil in a small, lidded frying pan and fry the duck, skin side down, for 5 minutes until golden. Turn the pieces, add the shallot to the pan and fry for a further 5 minutes.

3 Add the wine and garlic and crumble in the saffron. Cover and cook gently for 10 minutes (or a little longer if you prefer the duck well cooked).

4 Meanwhile, blend the pine nuts in a food processor with 3 tablespoons liquid taken from the pan to make a smooth paste.

5 Remove the duck and keep it warm. Add the pine nut paste to the pan with the raisins and sherry and cook, stirring, until the sauce is slightly thickened. Thinly slice the duck and divide it among small, warmed dishes. Drizzle with the sauce.

Griddled quail with almendras sauce *The small size of quail makes them perfect for little tapas tasters. A ridged griddle pan or heavy-based frying pan is ideal for cooking them, as is the barbecue.*

PREPARATION TIME: 15 minutes

COOKING TIME: 20 minutes

SERVES: 4–8

4 quails

2 tablespoons clear honey

1 tablespoon lemon juice

1 teaspoon finely chopped thyme

1 tablespoon olive oil

salt and pepper

Sauce

40 g (1½ oz) blanched almonds

yolks of 2 hard-boiled eggs

1 garlic clove, chopped

2 tablespoons medium sherry

150 ml (¼ pint) chicken stock

several sprigs of parsley

1 Use kitchen scissors or poultry shears to cut off the wing tips from the quails. Cut through each bird, either side of the backbone, and discard the bone. Cut through the breastbone to separate it into 2 pieces. With the skin side uppermost, press down firmly on each bird to flatten it. Push a long wooden skewer through each one to keep it flat and make it easier to handle.

2 Mix together the honey, lemon juice, thyme and a little salt and pepper and brush over the quails. Leave to stand.

3 Meanwhile, make the sauce. Toast the almonds until lightly browned and tip them into a food processor. Add the egg yolks and garlic and blend to a smooth paste. Add the sherry and stock and blend again until the mixture is completely smooth. Tear the parsley into the food processor and blend briefly until chopped. Turn the sauce into a small saucepan, ready to heat.

4 Brush a griddle or frying pan with the oil and gently fry the quails for about 10 minutes on each side until they are just beginning to char. Towards the end of the cooking time, heat the sauce and spoon it over the quails.

Game goujons with herb dressing

For these crisp, meaty bites, you can either spoon the dressing over little stacks of the goujons or serve it in small accompanying dishes to be used as a dip.

PREPARATION TIME: 25 minutes

COOKING TIME: 15 minutes

SERVES: 4–6

300 g (10 oz) skinless pheasant or partridge breast fillets

flour, for dusting

1 egg

100 g (3½ oz) fresh breadcrumbs

mild olive oil or sunflower oil, for frying

salt and pepper

Dressing

25 g (1 oz) butter

2 shallots, finely chopped

8 juniper berries, crushed

150 ml (¼ pint) chicken or game stock

1 tablespoon chopped oregano

4 tablespoons chopped parsley

1 teaspoon chopped thyme

1 tablespoon red wine vinegar

2 teaspoons clear honey

1 Cut the meat into thin strips. Season the flour and use it to coat the strips. Whisk the egg in a shallow dish and scatter the breadcrumbs on to a plate. Dip the game strips in the egg, then the breadcrumbs.

2 Make the dressing. Melt the butter in a frying pan and gently fry the shallots for 3 minutes until softened. Add the juniper berries and stock and bring to the boil. Cook until slightly reduced and thickened. Stir in the herbs, vinegar and honey then remove from the heat.

3 Heat oil to a depth of 2 cm (³/4 inch) in a frying pan until a few breadcrumbs sizzle on the surface. Fry half the strips for 2 minutes until golden. Remove with a slotted spoon to a plate lined with kitchen paper while you cook the remainder. Heat the herb dressing until bubbling and serve with the goujons.

Game goujons with herb dressing

Rabbit with Serrano ham and sage

For this recipe you'll need pieces of lean rabbit that are sufficiently large to beat thinly into portion-sized pieces. If only diced or small pieces of rabbit are available use chicken breast instead.

PREPARATION TIME: 15 minutes

COOKING TIME: about 5 minutes

SERVES: 6

275 g (9 oz) lean boneless rabbit

65 g (2½ oz) Serrano ham

10 large sage leaves

25 g (1 oz) butter

2 tablespoons olive oil

50 ml (2 fl oz) medium sherry

salt and pepper

1 Halve any larger pieces of meat so all the pieces are roughly the same size. Place them on a board between 2 layers of clingfilm and beat with a rolling pin until very thin. Season both sides of the meat with salt and pepper.

2 Tear the ham into pieces about the same size as the meat and place a piece of ham over each one, flattening them down to secure in place.

3 Finely shred the sage leaves. Melt the butter with the oil in a large frying pan. Add the chopped sage and fry for a few seconds. Add the meat, ham sides down, and fry for 2 minutes until lightly browned. Turn the pieces over and fry for a further minute or until cooked through. Remove the meat with a slotted spoon and keep it warm.

4 Add the sherry to the pan juices and let the mixture bubble up. Pour over the meat to serve.

Rabbit with pancetta and lentils

Lentils are so delicious because they absorb all the meaty flavours they're cooked with and soften quickly, thickening the juices. Also they don't need any soaking. This recipe is just as good with chicken or pork, as it is with rabbit.

PREPARATION TIME: 20 minutes

COOKING TIME: 45–55 minutes

SERVES: 6–8

100 g (3½ oz) Puy lentils

4 tablespoons olive oil

1 onion, finely chopped

75 g (3 oz) pancetta, diced

500 g (1 lb) lean rabbit, cut into small chunks

2 garlic cloves, crushed

1 cinnamon stick or a sprinkling of ground cinnamon

300 ml (½ pint) chicken or vegetable stock

175 g (6 oz) green cabbage, finely shredded

salt and pepper

1 Rinse the lentils thoroughly and put them in a saucepan with plenty of boiling water. Return to the boil, cook for 5 minutes, then drain.

2 Heat the oil in a saucepan and gently fry the onion and pancetta for 5 minutes. Add the rabbit and fry for 5 minutes until the meat is beginning to brown.

3 Stir in the garlic and cinnamon and add the stock. Bring to the boil, then reduce the heat to a gentle simmer. Add the lentils, cover with a lid and cook gently for 20–30 minutes until the rabbit and lentils are tender.

4 Stir in the cabbage and cook for a further 5 minutes. Check the seasoning and serve hot in little dishes.

Goat, Rioja and pepper hotpot

The flavour of goat is a little like lamb and the two are interchangeable in this recipe. The rich wine, paprika and olive juices are packed with meaty flavour and should be served with bread so none goes to waste.

PREPARATION TIME: 15 minutes

COOKING TIME: $1^1/_4$–$1^3/_4$ hours

SERVES: 6

400 g (13 oz) lean goat

25 g (1 oz) butter

2 tablespoons olive oil

1 red onion, chopped

2 red peppers, cored, deseeded and cut into chunks

2 garlic cloves, crushed

2 teaspoons mild sweet paprika

250 ml (8 fl oz) red Rioja

2 tablespoons Black Olive Paste (see page 25) or tapenade

salt and pepper

1 Trim any excess fat from the goat and cut the meat into small chunks. Season with salt and pepper.

2 Melt the butter with 1 tablespoon of oil in a flameproof casserole and fry the meat for 5 minutes until browned. Remove with a slotted spoon. Add the onion and peppers to the casserole with the remaining oil and fry gently for 10 minutes. Stir in the garlic and fry for a further minute.

3 Return the meat to the casserole along with the paprika, wine and olive paste or tapenade. Bring just to the boil, then reduce the heat and cover with a lid.

4 Cook the hotpot in a preheated oven, 160°C (325°F), Gas Mark 3, for 1–$1^1/_2$ hours until the meat is tender. Check the seasoning and serve hot in small dishes.

Sherried kidneys
Lambs' kidneys might not have a great deal of mass appeal, but they're a vital tapas ingredient in some regions of Spain. Cook them lightly so they remain tender and moist and serve with a full-flavoured red wine.

PREPARATION TIME: 10 minutes

COOKING TIME: 12–15 minutes

SERVES: 4

8 lambs' kidneys

2 tablespoons olive oil

1 small onion, finely chopped

100 ml (3½ fl oz) dry sherry

1 teaspoon grainy mustard

several sprigs of tarragon

4 small slices of walnut or grainy bread

salt and pepper

1 Halve the kidneys and snip out the white parts from the centres. Pat the kidneys dry on kitchen paper.

2 Heat the oil in a frying pan and gently fry the kidneys for about 2 minutes on each side until just cooked through. Remove with a slotted spoon and keep warm.

3 Add the onion to the pan and fry for 5 minutes until soft. Remove the pan from the heat and stir in 2 tablespoons of water then add the sherry and mustard. Return the pan to the heat and let the mixture bubble for a couple of minutes until reduced by about half. Pull the tarragon leaves from the stems and roughly chop. Add them to the pan with the kidneys and heat through gently for a minute.

4 Lightly toast the bread and pile the kidneys and sauce on top to serve.

Fish and seafood *Throughout Spain, fish and seafood, whether fresh, canned or salted, are important tapas ingredients. The Spanish eat far more fish than most other European countries, and their extensive choice is fished from the Mediterranean, Atlantic and beyond. This love of fish is reflected in a fabulous range of dishes, from the simple to the imaginative. Fresh anchovies, prawns, squid, mussels, hake and tuna are among the favourites and might be served simply with a garlicky, herby dressing or dipped in airy batters and deep-fried in olive oil. Salt cod is another favourite. Although it's not particularly attractive in its raw state, it can be transformed into some stunning dishes, from crisp fritters to creamy dips and robust stews, accompanied, more often than not, with a pot of aïoli.*

Salt cod with black beans

Simple bean stews are good make-ahead tapas dishes and reheat well. Aïoli is a classic partner to salt cod and is essential in this dish, its garlicky flavour melting into the bean juices.

PREPARATION TIME: 15 minutes, plus soaking

COOKING TIME: $1^3/4$–$2^1/4$ hours

SERVES: 6–8

200 g (7 oz) black beans,
  soaked overnight in cold water

250 g (8 oz) salt cod,
  soaked for 24–48 hours (see page 13)

4 tablespoons olive oil

2 onions, chopped

200 g (7 oz) small carrots, sliced

2 bay leaves

several sprigs of thyme

600 ml (1 pint) fish stock

pepper

Aïoli, to serve (see page 34)

1 Drain the beans, put them in a saucepan, cover with cold water and bring to the boil. Boil for 10 minutes, then drain. Tear the fish into small pieces, discarding the skin and bones.

2 Heat the oil in a large saucepan and fry the onions for 5 minutes until softened.

3 Add the drained beans, carrots, bay leaves, thyme and flaked fish. Add the stock and bring to the boil. Reduce the heat, cover with a lid and cook on the lowest heat for about $1^1/2$–2 hours or until the beans are very tender.

4 Season the stew with pepper and spoon it into small dishes. Top with spoonfuls of aïoli and serve hot.

Salt cod cakes with pepper caviar
Make these fishcakes any size you like. They can be little finger food morsels, in which case allow about three per serving, or larger fishcakes that you might want to serve on little plates with forks.

PREPARATION TIME: 30 minutes, plus soaking

COOKING TIME: 30 minutes

SERVES: 8

500 g (1 lb) floury potatoes, cut into chunks

500 g (1 lb) salt cod, soaked for 24–48 hours (see page 13)

2 garlic cloves, crushed

2 egg yolks

2 red peppers, cored and deseeded

2 teaspoons Thai fish sauce

mild olive oil, for frying

200 g (7 oz) crème fraîche

pepper

tiny sprigs of parsley, to garnish

1 Put the potatoes in a saucepan with the drained cod. Cover with cold water and bring to the boil. Reduce the heat and simmer gently until the potatoes are tender. Drain and return the potatoes to the pan, leaving the cod on a plate until it is cool enough to handle.

2 Flake the fish into small pieces, discarding any skin and bones.

3 Mash the potatoes with the garlic, egg yolks and a little pepper. Beat in the flaked fish. Take dessertspoonfuls of the mixture in your hands, shape it into balls and then flatten into little cakes. (If you're making larger fishcakes, divide the mash into 8 portions and shape each one into a cake.)

4 Chop the red pepper as finely as possible and stir in the fish sauce.

5 Heat a thin layer of oil in a large frying pan and fry the fishcakes, in batches, for 3–4 minutes until golden, turning once. Drain to a plate and leave to cool. Spoon a little crème fraîche on to each one and sprinkle with the pepper mixture. Serve garnished with parsley.

Hake fritters
These little fritters need to be cooked shortly before serving, but they are well worth the last-minute cooking. You can prepare them in advance to the end of step 2. Any other white fish, such as haddock, monkfish, pollock or cod, can be used instead of the hake.

PREPARATION TIME: 20 minutes

COOKING TIME: 10 minutes

SERVES: 6–8

300 g (10 oz) skinned hake fillets

125 g (4 oz) plain flour

50 g (2 oz) Manchego cheese, grated

2 tablespoons capers, chopped

2 tablespoons chopped parsley

2 tablespoons olive oil

1 egg, separated

mild olive oil or vegetable oil, for frying

salt and pepper

1 Check the fish for any stray bones, then cut the flesh into 2 cm (³/4 inch) pieces.

2 Mix the flour in a bowl with the cheese, capers, parsley and salt and pepper and make a well in the centre. Add the oil, egg yolk and 150 ml (¹/4 pint) water. Whisk the liquids together, gradually incorporating the flour to make a paste.

3 Whisk the egg white until peaking and fold it into the batter using a large metal spoon so the batter is lightened and aerated.

4 Heat oil to a depth of 5 cm (2 inches) in a large saucepan until a drop of the batter sizzles and turns golden in about 30 seconds.

5 Dip the pieces of fish in the batter then lower carefully into the oil, cooking about 10 pieces at a time, until puffed and golden. Drain on kitchen paper and keep warm while you cook the remaining fritters.

Tip Serve with Aïoli (see page 34) or Fresh Herb Oil (see page 25).

Marinated tuna with dill and capers

A fresh piece of tuna, steeped in a lemony marinade, makes a good prelude to more substantial tapas dishes. Serve on one large plate or on small, flat plates with bread to accompany.

PREPARATION TIME: 15 minutes, plus chilling

SERVES: 8

375 g (12 oz) fresh tuna, in one slender piece

finely grated rind of 1 lemon, plus 2 tablespoon juice

4 tablespoons chopped dill

3 tablespoons olive oil

½ teaspoon salt

2 teaspoons caster sugar

1 mild red chilli, thinly sliced

2 tablespoons capers or caperberries

1 Using a very sharp knife, cut the tuna as thinly as possible into delicate, wafer-thin slices. Arrange these in a single layer, but close together, on a large platter.

2 Mix together the lemon rind and juice, half the dill, the oil, salt, sugar and chilli and spoon the marinade all over the tuna, making sure all the slices are coated. Scatter with the remaining dill, pressing it firmly on to the fish.

3 Cover the dish loosely and chill for at least 1 hour. Scatter with the capers or caperberries to serve.

Tip Choose a long, thin piece of tuna so that it's easier to slice thinly. If you can only get a thick end of the fillet, cut it into two or three more manageable chunks first. Once prepared, the tuna can be chilled for several hours or overnight.

Seafood tartare tartlets

Rich and creamy, you'll probably only serve one per portion. Both filling and cases can be made in advance, but don't fill the cases until a couple of hours before serving.

PREPARATION TIME: 30 minutes, plus cooling

COOKING TIME: 25 minutes

MAKES: 12

350 g (11½ oz) lemon sole fillets or about 275 g (9 oz) skinned weight

3 tablespoons milk

250 g (8 oz) puff pastry

1 egg yolk

65 g (2½ oz) Aïoli (see page 34) or mayonnaise

75 g (3 oz) crème fraîche

25 g (1 oz) gherkins, finely chopped

25 g (1 oz) capers, drained, rinsed and finely chopped

15 g (½ oz) finely chopped parsley, plus extra to garnish

salt and pepper

1 Skin the sole fillets if necessary and put them in a frying pan with the milk and salt and pepper. Cook gently for about 5 minutes until cooked through.

2 Oil a large baking sheet. Thinly roll out the pastry, trim it to a 30 x 18 cm (12 x 7 inch) rectangle and transfer it to the baking sheet. Cut the pastry lengthways into 3 strips, then make 3 cuts widthways to make 12 rectangles.

3 Using the tip of a sharp knife, score each rectangle about 5 mm (¼ inch) from the edges. Brush the edges of each rectangle with egg yolk. Bake in a preheated oven, 220°C (425°F), Gas Mark 7, for 20 minutes until risen and golden. Cool on a wire rack.

4 Beat together the aïoli or mayonnaise and crème fraîche. Finely flake the fish and stir in with the gherkins, capers and parsley. Check the seasoning. Scoop the pastry centres out of the pastries to make cases and divide the filling among them. Scatter with extra parsley and pepper to garnish.

Mackerel escabeche

Like all mackerel dishes, this one's worth making only if the fish is absolutely fresh, then, once cooked it can be chilled overnight. Allow one fillet per portion, left whole or cut into pieces, with the juices spooned over and some bread for mopping up.

PREPARATION TIME: 20 minutes, plus chilling

COOKING TIME: 25 minutes

SERVES: 6–8

500 g (1 lb) mackerel fillets

1 tablespoon olive oil

2 shallots, thinly sliced

1 garlic clove, crushed

3 bay leaves

2 strips of pared orange rind, plus 50 ml (2 fl oz) juice

3 tablespoons chopped fennel or parsley

1 tablespoon grated fresh root ginger

100 ml (3½ fl oz) Pedro Ximenez or other sweet sherry

salt

1 Use tweezers to remove any stray bones from the mackerel then arrange the fillets, skin sides down, in a shallow ovenproof dish.

2 Heat the oil in a frying pan and gently fry the shallots until softened but not browned. Add the garlic and cook gently for 1 minute.

3 Add the bay leaves, orange rind and juice, fennel or parsley, ginger, sherry and a little salt and bring to the boil. Pour over the fish and cover with a lid or foil.

4 Cook the dish in a preheated oven, 180°C (350°F), Gas Mark 4, for 20 minutes or until the fish is just cooked through. Leave to cool then chill until ready to serve.

Stuffed piquillo peppers

Unlike fresh peppers, piquillo peppers are usually bought cooked and preserved in jars (see page 12). Their shape and size makes them perfect for stuffing with meat, vegetables or, as here, a rich paste of white fish and prawns.

PREPARATION TIME: 15 minutes, plus cooling

COOKING TIME: 5 minutes

SERVES: 8–12

275 g (9 oz) skinned white fish, such as hake, haddock, plaice, cod or red mullet

200 g (7 oz) raw peeled prawns

3 tablespoons milk

4 tablespoons Aïoli (see page 34), or use mayonnaise flavoured with 1 small crushed garlic clove

8 large or 12 small piquillo peppers, drained

1 tablespoon olive oil

squeeze of lemon juice and finely grated rind

salt and pepper

1 Check the fish for any bones and cut the flesh into chunky pieces. Put the fish in a small frying pan with the prawns and milk. Cover and cook gently for 5 minutes until cooked through. Leave to cool.

2 Drain the pan, reserving 3 tablespoons of the cooking liquid, and tip the fish and prawns into a food processor. Add the liquid and blend to a paste. Add the aïoli or mayonnaise and a little salt and pepper and blend until the mixture makes a fairly smooth paste.

3 Stuff the peppers with the seafood mixture, packing it in with a teaspoon. Arrange the peppers in a dish and drizzle with the oil and lemon juice. Scatter over the lemon rind and add a little salt and pepper. Cover and chill until ready to serve.

Variation You could use dressed crab instead of the prawns. Cook the white fish in the milk as above, allow to cool, then blend with 200 g (7 oz) crab meat.

Sardines in fresh tomato sauce

Make this recipe when you're sure you can get hold of very fresh sardines and tasty tomatoes. Serve one sardine per portion on a bed of the sauce.

PREPARATION TIME: 20 minutes

COOKING TIME: 55 minutes

SERVES: 8

4 tablespoons extra virgin olive oil

1 onion, finely chopped

2 garlic cloves, crushed

450 g (14½ oz) tomatoes, skinned and roughly chopped

2 tablespoons sun-dried tomato paste

2 tablespoons chopped oregano

8 large fresh sardines

salt and pepper

1 Heat 2 tablespoons of the oil in a frying pan and gently fry the onion for 5 minutes until softened. Add the garlic and fry gently for 1 minute.

2 Stir in the chopped tomatoes, tomato paste and oregano and bring to the boil. Reduce the heat and cook gently for about 10 minutes until the sauce is reduced and pulpy.

3 Meanwhile, scale the fish by running a thick bladed knife from tail to head to scrape off the scales. Work in a piece of crumpled paper or carrier bag to stop the scales from flying everywhere. Gut the fish and remove the heads. Wash and pat dry on kitchen paper.

4 Turn the tomato mixture into a shallow ovenproof dish and lay the fish on top. Drizzle with the remaining oil. Cover with foil and bake in a preheated oven, 180°C (350°F), Gas Mark 4, for 40 minutes until the fish is cooked through. Serve warm or cold.

Sardines in fresh tomato sauce

Beetroot and potato cakes with anchovies

Use ready-prepared marinated anchovy fillets from the deli counter or the ones on page 30. Alternatively, use halved canned or salted anchovy fillets.

PREPARATION TIME: 30 minutes

COOKING TIME: 20 minutes

MAKES: 16–18

200 g (7 oz) raw beetroot

450 g (14½ oz) waxy potatoes

25 g (1 oz) fresh root ginger, peeled and grated

2 tablespoons olive oil

200 g (7 oz) crème fraîche

16–18 marinated anchovy fillets

salt

sprigs of fennel or dill, to garnish

1 Coarsely grate the beetroot and potatoes. (This is most easily done using the grater attachment of a food processor.) Tip them out on to several thicknesses of kitchen paper. Cover with more kitchen paper and press down to remove as much moisture as possible. Turn into a bowl, add the ginger and plenty of salt and mix well.

2 Generously brush a baking sheet with a little of the oil. Take heaped dessertspoonfuls of the mixture, pat them into flat cakes and space slightly apart on the baking sheet. You should make 16–18 altogether.

3 Brush the cakes with the remaining oil and bake in a preheated oven, 200°C (400°F), Gas Mark 6, for 15 minutes. Turn them over with a palette knife and cook for a further 5 minutes.

4 Leave the cakes to cool slightly on the baking sheet. Top with spoonfuls of crème fraîche and an anchovy fillet and serve garnished with sprigs of fennel or dill.

Beetroot and potato cakes with anchovies

Spice-dusted prawns

Make this dish with only the freshest prawns and it'll be absolutely irresistible. Lightly spiced and fried, the prawns are served with a little pot of garlicky aïoli for dipping. This is finger food that needs finger bowls.

PREPARATION TIME: 10 minutes

COOKING TIME: 5 minutes

SERVES: 4–6

300 g (10 oz) raw, headless prawns

½ teaspoon ground cumin

½ teaspoon hot paprika

½ teaspoon celery salt

2 tablespoons olive oil

Aïoli, to serve (see page 34)

1 Peel the prawns if necessary (see page 14). You might like to leave on the tail shells so they can be used to hold the prawns for dipping.

2 Mix together the spices and celery salt and use the mixture to dust the prawns.

3 Heat the oil in a frying pan and gently fry the prawns for about 5 minutes, turning them when they're pink on the undersides. Cook them until they're just pink right through, but no longer or they'll start to toughen. Pile into little dishes and serve with aïoli.

Tip If you buy prawns with heads attached you will need about 450 g (14^1/$_2$ oz).

Prawns with garlicky crushed beans

White beans, such as cannellini, haricot or butter beans, make a perfect base for soaking up the sweet juices from the prawn sauce. Lightly mash them so they retain a bit of texture.

PREPARATION TIME: 10 minutes

COOKING TIME: 10 minutes

SERVES: 8–10

4 tablespoons olive oil

1 large onion, finely chopped

3 garlic cloves, crushed

2 x 400 g (13 oz) cans cannellini, haricot or butter beans, drained

100 ml (3½ fl oz) vegetable or fish stock

400 g (13 oz) shelled raw prawns

½ teaspoon mild sweet paprika

2 tablespoons sun-dried tomato paste

1 tablespoon chopped oregano

2 teaspoons clear honey

salt and pepper

1 Heat 2 tablespoons of the oil in a saucepan and gently fry the onion for 5 minutes. Add the garlic and fry for a further minute.

2 Tip in the beans and use a potato masher to crush them. Add the stock and plenty of black pepper and leave in the pan, ready to reheat.

3 Dust the prawns with the paprika and a little salt. Heat the remaining oil in a frying pan and fry the prawns lightly on both sides until cooked through. Stir in the tomato paste, oregano, honey and 2 tablespoons water.

4 Heat the beans in the saucepan until just hot and heat the prawns until the juices start to bubble. Spoon the bean mixture into small dishes, pile the prawns on top and pour over the cooking juices.

Prawns with whole chillies and garlic

Freshly cooked prawns, chillies and garlic cloves give the olive oil plenty of flavour, so serve this dish with bread so that you don't waste it. An accompanying pot of aïoli provides an extra burst of garlicky flavour.

PREPARATION TIME: 20 minutes

COOKING TIME: 5 minutes

SERVES: 6

450 g (14½ oz) small whole raw prawns

6 garlic cloves

100 ml (3½ fl oz) olive oil

6 whole dried red chillies

salt

1 Peel the prawns, leaving the tails intact (see page 14). Cut the garlic cloves in half.

2 Heat the oil in a frying pan and gently heat the garlic cloves and chillies for a couple of minutes to flavour the oil. Don't fry them over too high a heat or the garlic will burn. Add the prawns and cook gently, turning once, until they have just turned pink. Avoid overcooking or they will start to toughen.

3 Transfer the prawns to small serving dishes and spoon over the oil, making sure that each dish contains a chilli and a garlic clove. Serve sprinkled with salt.

Black rice with squid

Most squid is bought ready prepared, so it won't have the ink sacs that give this dish its distinctive colour. Instead, use sachets of black squid ink, which are available from fish suppliers or some delicatessens.

PREPARATION TIME: 20 minutes

COOKING TIME: 40 minutes

SERVES: 8–10

400 g (13 oz) prepared squid (see page 15)

100 ml (3½ fl oz) olive oil

1 onion, chopped

3 garlic cloves, crushed

300 g (10 oz) paella rice

150 ml (¼ pint) white wine

3 tomatoes, skinned and chopped

1 teaspoon hot paprika

several sprigs of thyme

900 ml (1½ pints) fish stock

3 x 4 g (¼ oz) sachets squid ink

salt and pepper

4 tablespoons chopped parsley, to serve

1 Thickly slice the squid bodies if they are large then dry the squid on kitchen paper.

2 Heat half the oil in a large frying pan and fry the squid for about 5 minutes until it is beginning to colour. Remove with a slotted spoon and set aside. Add the onion to the pan and fry for 5 minutes. Add the garlic and fry for another minute.

3 Stir in the rice and cook for 2 minutes. Pour in the wine and let the mixture bubble until the liquid evaporates.

4 Add the tomatoes, paprika, thyme and stock and bring to the boil. Reduce the heat and cook gently, stirring frequently, for about 20 minutes, until the rice is just tender, adding a dash more stock if the mixture becomes dry.

5 Mix the squid ink with 1 tablespoon hot water and add to the pan with the squid. Cook, stirring, until the rice has coloured. Stir in the remaining oil and serve scattered with parsley.

Tip If the squid comes with ink sacs intact, cut open the sacs and dilute the ink with a little water.

Crisp fried seafood

Use a medley of whatever suitable fish you can get hold of for this recipe. Squid, whitebait, small sprats or cubes of any firm white fish are ideal.

PREPARATION TIME: 20 minutes

COOKING TIME: 5 minutes

SERVES: 4–6

500 g (1 lb) mixed seafood, such as whitebait, skinned white fish and prepared squid (see page 15)

1 spring onion, trimmed

1 mild red chilli, thinly sliced

1 garlic clove, finely chopped

2 tablespoons chopped parsley

100 g (3½ oz) semolina flour

½ teaspoon mild sweet paprika

mild olive oil or sunflower oil, for deep-frying

salt and pepper

lemon or lime wedges, to serve

1 Cut the white fish into small chunks. Slice the squid into rings and pat dry on kitchen paper, with the tentacles and any other seafood you might be using.

2 Finely chop the spring onion and mix it with the chilli, garlic, parsley and salt.

3 Mix together the semolina flour and paprika. Season lightly with salt and pepper and use the mixture to coat the fish. Heat oil to a depth of 5 cm (2 inches) in a large saucepan or deep-fat fryer until a 1 cm (1/2 inch) cube of bread sizzles on the surface and browns in 30 seconds.

4 Fry the fish in batches for 30–60 seconds until crisp and golden. Drain on kitchen paper and keep warm while you cook the remainder. Serve in little dishes, sprinkled with the spring onion and herb mixture and accompanied by the lemon or lime wedges.

Crisp fried seafood

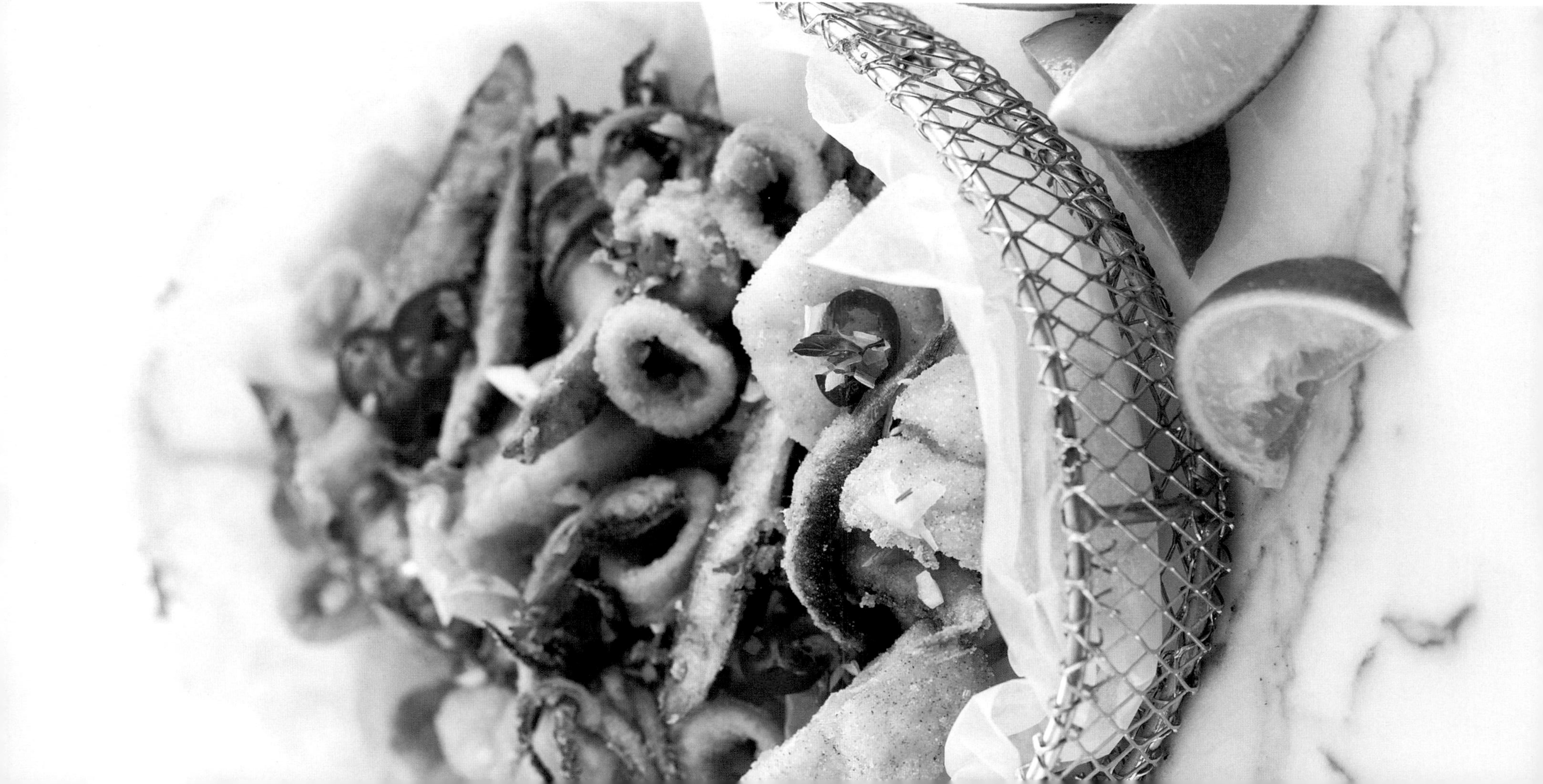

Stuffed squid
Make these several hours in advance to avoid last-minute preparation because they're quite fiddly. Choose smallish squid but not so small that they're impossible to stuff.

PREPARATION TIME: 30 minutes

COOKING TIME: about 15 minutes

SERVES: 6–8

500 g (1 lb) small squid tubes,
   each 10–12 cm (4–5 inches) long

5 tablespoons olive oil

1 onion, finely chopped

2 garlic cloves, crushed

1 medium courgette, grated

½ teaspoon saffron threads

75 g (3 oz) blanched almonds, coarsely ground

25 g (1 oz) sultanas, chopped

1 tablespoon lemon juice

salt and pepper

1 Pat the squid dry on kitchen paper. Heat 2 tablespoons of oil in a frying pan and gently fry the onion for 5 minutes. Add the garlic and courgette and fry for a further 3–4 minutes until the courgette softens.

2 Crumble in the saffron and add the almonds. Cook gently, stirring, for 2 minutes. Stir in the sultanas and a little salt and pepper. Leave to cool.

3 Pack the mixture into the squid using a small teaspoon and secure the open ends with short wooden skewers or cocktail sticks. (Leave a bit of space at the top so the filling doesn't burst out.) Season with plenty of pepper.

4 Brush a heavy-based frying pan with another tablespoon of the oil and fry the squid for about 5 minutes, turning once. Transfer to small plates. Mix the remaining oil with the lemon juice and plenty of black pepper and drizzle over to serve.

Octopus with garlic dressing

Buy prepared octopus at least a couple of days before you need it so that you can freeze it for 48 hours before cooking. This tenderizes the flesh, which might otherwise be extremely tough to eat. Once made, the dish will keep for a couple of days in the refrigerator.

PREPARATION TIME: 10 minutes, plus cooling

COOKING TIME: $1^1/2$ hours

SERVES: 6–8

1 onion, cut into wedges

1 teaspoon whole cloves

500 g (1 lb) prepared octopus

6 tablespoons extra virgin olive oil

2 garlic cloves, crushed

4 tablespoons chopped parsley

1 teaspoon white wine vinegar

salt and pepper

1 Put the onion, cloves and 1 tablespoon salt in a large saucepan and add 2 litres ($3^1/2$ pints) cold water. Bring to the boil. Using tongs, dip the octopus in and out of the water about 4 times, returning the water to the boil before re-dipping, then immerse the octopus completely in the water. (This helps to make the flesh tender.) If there are several pieces of octopus, dip them one at a time.

2 Reduce the heat and cook the octopus very gently for 1 hour. Check to see whether it's tender, if necessary cooking it for another 15–30 minutes. Leave it to cool in the liquid.

3 Drain the octopus and cut the flesh into bite-sized pieces. Turn them into a bowl.

4 Mix the oil with the garlic, parsley, vinegar and salt and pepper and add to the bowl. Mix well, cover and chill for several hours or overnight. Serve with bread for mopping up the juices.

Steamed mussels with pepper dressing

Serve these mussels steaming hot in little dishes with small forks for scooping them out with the dressing. The recipe also works well with small clams.

PREPARATION TIME: 20 minutes

COOKING TIME: 12 minutes

SERVES: 6–8

4 tablespoons olive oil

1 green pepper, cored, deseeded and finely chopped

1 medium-strength green chilli, deseeded and finely chopped

1 small red onion, finely chopped

3 garlic cloves, crushed

finely grated rind of 1 lime or lemon, plus 1 tablespoon juice

1 teaspoon clear honey

4 tablespoons dry sherry

1 kg (2 lb) fresh mussels

salt

1 Heat 2 tablespoons of the oil in a small frying pan and gently fry the pepper, chilli and onion for about 5 minutes until very soft. Add the garlic and cook for a further 2 minutes. Remove the pan from the heat, stir in the lime or lemon rind and juice, honey and sherry and season with a little salt.

2 Clean the mussels, discarding any damaged shells or open ones that do not close when tapped sharply with a knife (see page 14).

3 Heat 2 tablespoons water in a large saucepan, tip in the mussels and cover with a tight-fitting lid. Steam for about 5 minutes, shaking the pan frequently until the shells have opened.

4 Tip the mussels into a sieve or colander to drain off the cooking liquor. Return the mussels to the pan, discarding any shells that have not opened. Add the remaining oil and stir the mussels around until they are coated. Spoon over the sauce and pile into little dishes.

Steamed mussels with pepper dressing

Scallops with morcilla

This dish looks stunning served in the rounded shells of the scallops, which make natural, perfectly sized little tapas dishes. If using ready-shelled scallops, serve in small dishes.

PREPARATION TIME: 10 minutes

COOKING TIME: 5 minutes

SERVES: 6

6 scallops, preferably in their shells

25 g (1 oz) morcilla

2 tablespoons olive oil

1 spring onion, finely sliced

1 teaspoon chopped lemon thyme

salt and pepper

1 Prepare the scallops (see page 15). Pat the scallops dry on kitchen paper and season lightly with salt and pepper. Finely chop or break the morcilla into small pieces.

2 Heat the oil in a small frying pan and gently fry the scallops for 1 minute on each side. Transfer them to the cleaned shells or to small, warmed serving dishes.

3 Add the spring onion, lemon thyme and morcilla to the pan and heat gently, stirring, for 1 minute. Season lightly with salt and pepper and spoon over the scallops with the cooking juices to serve.

Chilli clams with romesco sauce

Use small, smooth-shelled clams for this recipe rather than the larger ridged ones that tend to be much chewier. The clams are delicious served with little pots of the sauce, or if you prefer, a garlicky aïoli.

PREPARATION TIME: 10 minutes

COOKING TIME: 10 minutes

SERVES: 6–8

1 kg (2 lb) fresh clams

½ teaspoon saffron threads

3 tablespoons olive oil

2 shallots, finely chopped

1 medium-strength red chilli, deseeded and thinly sliced

2 tablespoons sherry vinegar

Romesco Sauce, to serve (see page 35)

1 Clean the clams, discarding any damaged shells or open ones that do not close when tapped sharply with a knife (see page 14).

2 Crumble the saffron into a bowl and add 1 tablespoon boiling water. Leave to stand for 5 minutes.

3 Heat the oil in a saucepan or large, lidded frying pan and fry the shallots for 5 minutes until softened. Stir in the chilli, vinegar, saffron and its liquid and cook until bubbling.

4 Tip the clams into the pan and cover with a lid. Cook for about 5 minutes, shaking the pan frequently, until the shells have opened.

5 Turn the clams into small, warmed dishes, discarding any shells that remain closed. Spoon over the cooking juices and serve warm with the Romesco sauce.

Paella cakes
These delicious tapas are made using a firm paella mixture, shaped into little balls and deep-fried in breadcrumbs. Cook the mixture, leave it to cool and then shape and coat with breadcrumbs, leaving the frying until shortly before serving.

PREPARATION TIME: 40 minutes, plus cooling

COOKING TIME: 30 minutes

MAKES: 20

200 g (7 oz) prepared squid (see page 15)

3 tablespoons olive oil

½ teaspoon crushed dried chillies

3 garlic cloves, crushed

175 g (6 oz) paella rice

500 ml (17 fl oz) chicken or vegetable stock

1 teaspoon saffron threads, crumbled

2 piquillo peppers, chopped

50 g (2 oz) fresh or frozen peas

1 skinless cooked chicken breast, chopped

2 eggs

100 g (3½ oz) fresh breadcrumbs

sunflower oil, for deep-frying

1 Thinly slice the squid, including the tentacles (if used) and pat dry on kitchen paper. Heat the oil in a large frying pan and gently fry the squid, chillies and garlic for 3 minutes.

2 Add the rice and cook, stirring, for 1 minute. Add the stock and saffron and bring to the boil. Reduce the heat and cook gently for 15–20 minutes or until the stock has been absorbed and the rice is tender and sticky. Cool in a bowl.

3 Add the peppers, peas, chicken and 1 egg and mix well. Shape the mixture into 20 small balls (wet your hands to prevent the mixture from sticking).

4 Lightly beat the remaining egg on a plate and put the breadcrumbs on another. Roll the balls in the egg and then the breadcrumbs, then clench them quite firmly to make sure they are compact and not likely to fall apart.

5 Heat oil to a depth of 5 cm (2 inches) in a large saucepan or deep-fat fryer until a few breadcrumbs sizzle on the surface. Fry the paella balls for about 3 minutes, in 2 batches, until they are crisp and golden. Drain on kitchen paper and serve.

Vegetables *Spain's plentiful supplies of fresh, colourful, sweetly flavoured vegetables offer a feast of resources for tapas dishes. Perfectly ripe tomatoes, peppers, cucumbers, aubergines, courgettes, artichokes, spinach and onions are sufficiently flavour packed to need few additional ingredients. Vegetable tapas might be as simple as lightly cooked vegetables with a pot of aïoli, or a more lengthily cooked dish, such as Patatas Bravas (see page 117) or Samfaina (see page 120). Vegetable soups, either chilled or hot, make delicious little tasters, and both Garlic and Almond Soup (see page 112) and Gazpacho (see page 113) are real tapas classics.*

Garlic and almond soup

Small portions of this rich and creamy soup, served in small glasses, are ideal for tapas, while larger portions make a great summer starter. Set the soup off with a light sprinkling of vibrant orange paprika.

PREPARATION TIME: 10 minutes, plus standing and chilling

SERVES: 8–10

75 g (3 oz) white bread, crusts removed

5 tablespoons milk

125 g (4 oz) blanched almonds

3 garlic cloves, chopped

1 tablespoon sherry vinegar

4 tablespoons extra virgin olive oil, plus extra to serve

salt and pepper

mild sweet paprika, to sprinkle

1 Tear the bread into pieces and put it into a bowl with the milk. Leave to soak for 10 minutes.

2 Blitz the almonds in a food processor until finely ground. Add the bread and milk, garlic and vinegar and blend to a smooth paste. Add 400 ml (14 fl oz) cold water and blend again to give a milky consistency.

3 Gradually pour in the oil until blended. Season with salt and pepper and chill for at least an hour.

4 Pour the soup into small glasses and use a spoon to drizzle over a little extra oil. Sprinkle lightly with paprika and serve.

Gazpacho

When it is served as a starter this fresh-tasting chilled soup is garnished with ingredients such as chopped peppers and onions, croutons and ice cubes, but tapas portions are best left simple – perhaps with just a sprinkling of black pepper or finely chopped parsley.

PREPARATION TIME: 10 minutes, plus chilling

SERVES: 12

1 kg (2 lb) well-flavoured tomatoes, skinned and roughly chopped

1 cucumber, skinned and roughly chopped

1 red pepper, cored, deseeded and roughly chopped

75 g (3 oz) white bread, crusts removed

2 garlic cloves, chopped

½ small red onion, roughly chopped

2 tablespoons wine or sherry vinegar

5 tablespoons extra virgin olive oil

salt and pepper

1 Put the tomatoes, cucumber and pepper in a bowl. Tear the bread into pieces and add it to the bowl with the garlic, onion and vinegar.

2 Blend the ingredients, in batches, in a food processor until completely smooth, scraping the mixture down from the sides of the bowl.

3 Pour the soup into a clean bowl, whisk in the oil and season to taste with salt and pepper. If the soup is very thick, whisk in a little cold water. Cover and chill for at least an hour before serving. Serve in small cups or glasses.

Griddled stuffed pittas

These delicious treats combine a classic Mediterranean mixture of pine nuts, spinach and raisins with pitta breads, which were introduced into Spanish cooking by the Moors.

PREPARATION TIME: 15 minutes

COOKING TIME: 10 minutes

SERVES: 6

6 small round pitta breads

2 tablespoons olive oil

50 g (2 oz) pine nuts

2 garlic cloves, crushed

300 g (10 oz) young spinach

75 g (3 oz) Manchego cheese, grated

40 g (1½ oz) raisins, chopped

salt and pepper

1 Make a slit along one side of each pitta bread and push the knife inside to make a cavity.

2 Heat the oil in a frying pan and gently fry the pine nuts and garlic for 2 minutes until just beginning to colour. Add the spinach and turn it in the pan until it has wilted. Stir in the cheese and raisins and sprinkle with a little salt and pepper. Remove the pan from the heat and mix the ingredients well together.

3 Pack the mixture into the pitta breads, spreading it to the edges in an even layer.

4 Toast the pitta breads in a panini machine or use a griddle or heavy-based frying pan until lightly browned on both sides. (If you are using a griddle or frying pan, press the breads flat in the pan with a fish slice.) Leave to cool slightly, then halve each pitta and serve warm.

Tip Use very fresh pitta breads so that they don't crack open during cooking.

Courgette fritters with vodka-flamed tomatoes

Polenta gives the courgettes a crispy coating that provides a savoury contrast to the tomatoes. It's sometimes sold as cornmeal, particularly in health food stores.

PREPARATION TIME: 25 minutes

COOKING TIME: 20–25 minutes

SERVES: 6

3 tablespoons olive oil

1 shallot, finely chopped

½ teaspoon hot paprika

375 g (12 oz) cherry tomatoes, halved

½ teaspoon caster sugar

3 tablespoons vodka

Fritters

2 large courgettes

2 tablespoons plain flour

1½ teaspoons celery salt

1 egg, beaten

75 g (3 oz) polenta or cornmeal

mild olive oil or sunflower oil, for frying

1 Heat the oil in a frying pan and gently fry the shallot for 5 minutes until softened. Stir in the paprika, cherry tomatoes and sugar and cook gently, stirring, for about 5 minutes until the tomatoes start to soften.

2 Add the vodka to the pan and light with a taper or long match to ignite. When the flames die down, set the pan to one side while you prepare the courgettes. (Don't worry if the vodka doesn't ignite, because the alcohol will burn off if you cook it for a couple of minutes.)

3 Make the fritters. Cut the courgettes into long, thin, diagonal slices, each slice about 5 mm (¼ inch) thick. Toss the flour with the celery salt on a plate. Tip the egg on to a small plate and the polenta on to a third plate.

4 Toss the courgette slices in the flour then the egg and finally the polenta.

5 Heat a thin layer of oil in a large frying pan and gently fry the courgettes, in 2 batches, for 2–3 minutes on each side until golden and tender. Drain on kitchen paper. Serve several slices per portion, topped with a spoonful of the tomatoes.

Patatas bravas

This version of the classic Spanish dish uses a thick, rich tomato sauce, while the potatoes retain their crisp, appetizing texture. Any type of flavoursome potato will give good results.

PREPARATION TIME: 20 minutes

COOKING TIME: 25 minutes

SERVES: 6

800 g (1 lb 10 oz) potatoes

5 tablespoons olive oil

1 red onion, chopped

2 bay leaves

½ teaspoon hot paprika

2 garlic cloves, crushed

4 tomatoes, skinned and chopped

2 tablespoons sun-dried tomato paste

3 tablespoons flat leaf parsley, roughly chopped

salt

1 Cut the potatoes into small chunks. Heat 3 tablespoons of the oil in a large frying pan. Add the potatoes and a pinch of salt and fry gently, stirring frequently, for 15 minutes until golden.

2 Meanwhile, in a separate pan heat the remaining oil and fry the onion with the bay leaves for 5 minutes. Add the paprika and garlic and fry for a further minute.

3 Stir in the tomatoes, tomato paste, half the parsley and 2 tablespoons water. Cover and cook for 8–10 minutes, stirring occasionally to break up the tomatoes.

4 Add the tomato sauce to the potatoes and cook for a further 5 minutes, adding a dash of water if the sauce loses its juiciness. Check the seasoning and serve hot, sprinkled with parsley.

Vegetables **117**

Stuffed baby aubergines

Take the opportunity to make these little treats when you see miniature aubergines in the shops because they're a perfect size for tapas. Serve one or two per portion.

PREPARATION TIME: 25 minutes

COOKING TIME: 30 minutes

SERVES: 8–16

8 baby aubergines

3 tablespoons olive oil

1 small onion, chopped

1 celery stick, chopped

2 garlic cloves, crushed

2 teaspoons cumin seeds, crushed

½ teaspoon ground turmeric

2 tablespoons grated fresh root ginger

125 g (4 oz) canned chickpeas, drained

40 g (1½ oz) Manchego cheese, grated

salt and pepper

1 Put the aubergines on a baking sheet and bake in a preheated oven, 190°C (375°F), Gas Mark 5, for 10 minutes until softened. Leave to cool slightly, then cut them in half lengthways. Scoop out the centres, leaving a thin shell, and chop the scooped-out flesh. Return the shells to the roasting tin, cut sides up. Brush with 1 tablespoon of the oil and season lightly with salt and pepper.

2 Heat the remaining oil in a frying pan and gently fry the onion and celery for 5 minutes. Add the garlic, spices and chopped aubergine and fry for a further 3 minutes.

3 Lightly crush the chickpeas by mashing them against the side of a bowl or by whizzing them briefly in a food processor. Add to the pan, season with salt and pepper and mix well.

4 Pile the mixture into the aubergine shells and sprinkle with the cheese. Return the aubergines to the oven for a further 10 minutes. Serve warm.

Stuffed baby aubergines

Samfaina

This well-flavoured blend of colourful Mediterranean vegetables is perfect with cheese or meat tapas. It can be served in little dishes or, more interestingly, shaped in little moulds, turned out on to plates and drizzled with herb oil.

PREPARATION TIME: 20 minutes, plus cooling and chilling

COOKING TIME: 30 minutes

SERVES: 6

4 tablespoons extra virgin olive oil

1 medium aubergine, cut into small chunks

2 red peppers, cored, deseeded and cut into small chunks

1 orange or yellow pepper, cored, deseeded and cut into small chunks

1 onion, chopped

2 garlic cloves, crushed

4 tomatoes, skinned and chopped

salt and pepper

Fresh Herb Oil, to serve (see page 25)

1 Heat 2 tablespoons of the oil in a large frying pan and gently fry the aubergine, stirring frequently, for 10 minutes until browned. Slide on to a plate.

2 Add the peppers and onion to the pan with the remaining oil and fry gently for 5 minutes.

3 Return the aubergine to the pan with the garlic and tomatoes. Cover with a lid or foil and cook gently for 15 minutes until the vegetables are soft and pulpy. Remove the lid and let the mixture bubble for a couple of minutes to boil off any juices. Season to taste and leave to cool slightly.

4 Line 6 dariole moulds, each with a 125 ml (4 fl oz) capacity, with clingfilm and pack in the mixture, pressing it down with the back of a spoon. Chill until ready to serve.

5 Invert the moulds on to small plates and peel away the clingfilm. Drizzle with the herb oil to serve.

Mushrooms with broad bean purée

Use large flat mushrooms, which will make perfect, slightly cupped containers for the delicious, brightly coloured purée. It can be made ahead, covered and chilled, ready for popping in the oven to reheat.

PREPARATION TIME: 20 minutes

COOKING TIME: 15 minutes

SERVES: 6

6 large flat mushrooms

50 g (2 oz) butter, melted

2 garlic cloves, crushed

150 g (5 oz) broad beans

50 g (2 oz) light soft cheese

2 teaspoons chopped mint

5 g (½ oz) chives

1 tablespoon lemon-infused olive oil

salt and pepper

1 Peel the mushrooms and place them, stalk sides up, in a shallow ovenproof dish. Mix the butter with the garlic and a little salt and pepper and brush over the mushrooms. Bake in a preheated oven, 200°C (400°F), Gas Mark 6, for 10 minutes.

2 Meanwhile, cook the broad beans in plenty of boiling water until tender. Drain and cool slightly under running water. Take about a quarter of the beans and pop them out of their shells.

3 Put the remaining beans in a food processor with the cheese, mint, half the chives and salt and pepper and blend until smooth, scraping the mixture down from the sides of the bowl.

4 Spoon the mixture on to the mushrooms. Scatter with the shelled beans and drizzle with the oil. Return to the oven for a further 5 minutes. Served scattered with the remaining chives.

Chilli and pepper terrine
This colourful layering of red and yellow peppers looks fabulous when it's cut into slices. It keeps well in the refrigerator, so you can make it up to a day in advance.

PREPARATION TIME: 30 minutes, plus cooling

COOKING TIME: 30 minutes

SERVES: 8

4 red peppers

4 yellow peppers

50 g (2 oz) blanched almonds

25 g (1 oz) basil leaves

1 teaspoon harissa paste

2 tablespoons mild olive oil

2 teaspoons clear honey

salt

1 Put the whole peppers in a roasting tin and cook in a preheated oven, 200°C (400°F), Gas Mark 6, for 30 minutes or until they are soft and the skins are browned. Turn them into a bowl, cover with clingfilm and leave to cool.

2 Meanwhile, blitz the almonds in a food processor until ground. Add the basil leaves, harissa, oil, honey and a little salt and blend to a smooth paste, scraping the mixture down from the sides of the bowl.

3 Pull the stalks from the peppers and peel away the skins. Drain the juices from inside the peppers and cut them in half, discarding the seeds. Dry the peppers between several sheets of kitchen paper.

4 Line a 500 g (1 lb) loaf tin with clingfilm. Place a single layer of yellow pepper in the base, cutting to fit where necessary. Spread with a teaspoonful of the paste. Cover with a layer of red pepper and spread with more paste. Repeat the layering, finishing with a layer of peppers. Chill until ready to serve.

5 Invert on to a board and peel away the clingfilm. Use a sharp knife to cut the terrine into squares.

Goats' cheese and pepper tarts

For a quick version of this recipe, use ready-made shortcrust pastry and replace the pepper filling with chopped roasted peppers from the deli counter.

PREPARATION TIME: 40 minutes, plus chilling

COOKING TIME: 20 minutes

MAKES: 12

200 g (7 oz) plain flour

1 teaspoon mild sweet paprika

½ teaspoon salt

75 g (3 oz) butter

1 hot guindilla (pickled green pepper), thinly sliced

salt and pepper

Filling

2 tablespoons olive oil

2 green peppers, cored, deseeded and finely chopped

2 garlic cloves, crushed

2 tablespoons raisins, chopped

150 g (5 oz) soft fresh goats' cheese

1 Put the flour, paprika and salt in a bowl. Add the butter, cut into small pieces, and rub it in with the fingertips until the mixture resembles fine breadcrumbs. Add cold water, 1–2 tablespoons, to mix to a dough. Knead lightly until smooth. Wrap and chill for 30 minutes.

2 Thinly roll out the dough on a lightly floured surface and cut out 12 rounds using a 7.5 cm (3 inch) cutter. Press the rounds into the sections of a tartlet tin, prick the bases with a fork and chill for 20 minutes. Bake in a preheated oven, 200°C (400°F), Gas Mark 6, for 15 minutes. (Leave the oven on.)

3 Make the filling. Heat the oil in a frying pan and gently fry the peppers for about 10 minutes until very soft. Stir in the garlic and raisins and cook for 2 minutes.

4 Season the goats' cheese with black pepper and spoon into the tartlets. Top with the peppers and bake for a further 5 minutes. Serve scattered with hot pepper slices.

Goats' cheese and pepper tarts

Index

Acknowledgements

Special photography: © **Octopus Publishing Group Ltd**/Stephen Conroy

Editor Charlotte Macey
Executive Art Editor Penny Stock
Design Geoff Borin
Senior Production Controller Martin Croshaw
Food Stylist Joanna Farrow
Props Stylist Liz Hippisley